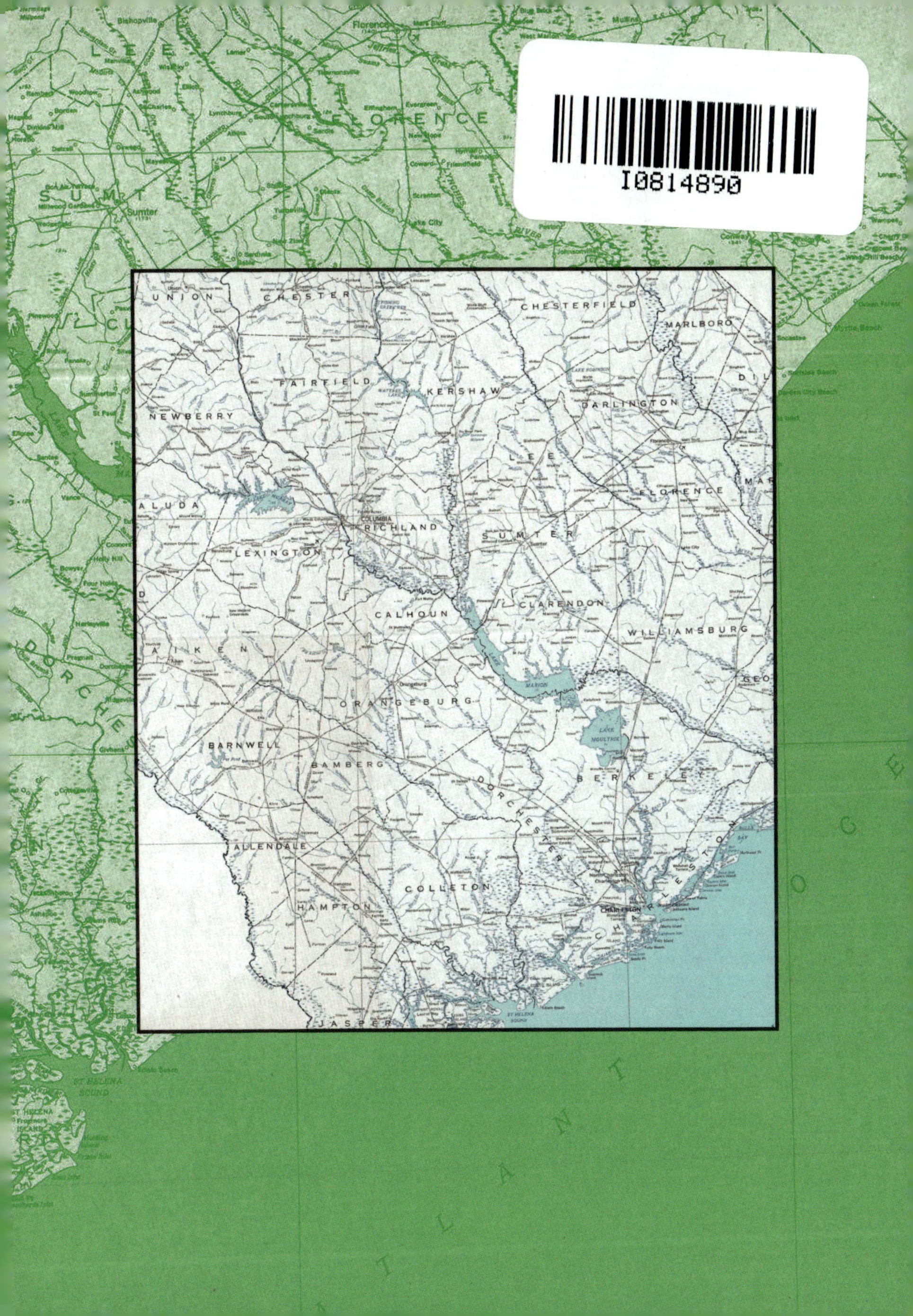

LEE
FLORENCE
SUMTER
Sumter
Bishopville
Florence
Lake City
UNION
CHESTER
CHESTERFIELD
MARLBORO
FAIRFIELD
KERSHAW
NEWBERRY
DARLINGTON
LEE
FLORENCE
ALUDA
COLUMBIA
RICHLAND
SUMTER
LEXINGTON
CALHOUN
CLARENDON
WILLIAMSBURG
AIKEN
MARION
ORANGEBURG
BARNWELL
BAMBERG
DORCHESTER
BERKELEY
ALLENDALE
COLLETON
HAMPTON
CHARLESTON
JASPER
ATLANT
OCE

LEE
FLORENCE
MARION
HORRY
SUMTER
CLARENDON
WILLIAMSBURG
GEORGETOWN
BERKELEY
DORCHESTER
CHARLESTON
ATLANTIC OCEAN
LAKE MARION
LAKE MOULTRIE
Bishopville
Florence
Mars Bluff
Mullins
Marion
West Marion
Lamar
Timmonsville
Effingham
Evergreen
Lynchburg
South Lynchburg
Sardis
New Hope
Pamplico
Sumter
Turbeville
Olanta
Scranton
Lake City
Conway
Loris
Galivants Ferry
Aynor
Horry
Homewood
Toddville
Dongola
Bucksville
Socastee
Myrtle Beach
Surfside Beach
Garden City Beach
Murrells Inlet
Brookgreen
Litchfield Beach
Pawleys Island
Manning
Paxville
Alcolu
Summerton
Kingstree
Hemingway
Johnsonville
Cadet
Greeleyville
Lane
Andrews
Georgetown
Maryville
Santee
Eutawville
Vance
Holly Hill
Pineville
Russellville
St Stephens
Jamestown
Bonneau
Moncks Corner
Macbeth
Harleyville
Ridgeville
Summerville
Goose Creek
Ladson
North Charleston
Charleston Hts
CHARLESTON
Mount Pleasant
Sullivans Island
Isle of Palms
McClellanville
Awendaw
Cape Island
Cape Romain
BULLS BAY
Folly Beach
Folly Island
Morris Island
JAMES ISLAND
JOHNS ISLAND
WADMALAW ISLAND
Rockville
Seabrook Island
EDISTO ISLAND
Edisto Beach
ST HELENA SOUND
ST HELENA ISLAND
Hunting Island
North Santee
South Santee
CAT ISLAND
North Inlet
WINYAH BAY
WACCAMAW NECK
Santee Pt

SOUTH CAROLINA COCKTAILS

An Elegant Collection of Over 100 Recipes Inspired by the Palmetto State

STEPHANIE BURT

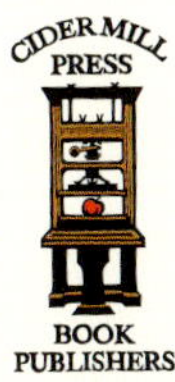

SOUTH CAROLINA COCKTAILS

Published by Cider Mill Press, an imprint of HarperCollins Focus LLC,
501 Nelson Place, Nashville, TN 37214 USA.

13-Digit ISBN: 978-1-40034-903-6
10-Digit ISBN: 1-40034-903-6

Books published by Cider Mill Press Book Publishers are available at special discounts for bulk purchases in the United States by corporations, institutions, and other organizations. For more information, please contact the publisher.

cidermillpress.com

HarperCollins Publishers, Macken House, 39/40 Mayor Street Upper,
Dublin 1, D01 C9W8, Ireland (https://www.harpercollins.com)

Typography: Copperplate, Magno Serif Variable, Sackers Gothic Std, Warnock Pro

Image Credits on page 260

Printed in India

25 26 27 28 29 REP 5 4 3 2 1

First Edition

CONTENTS

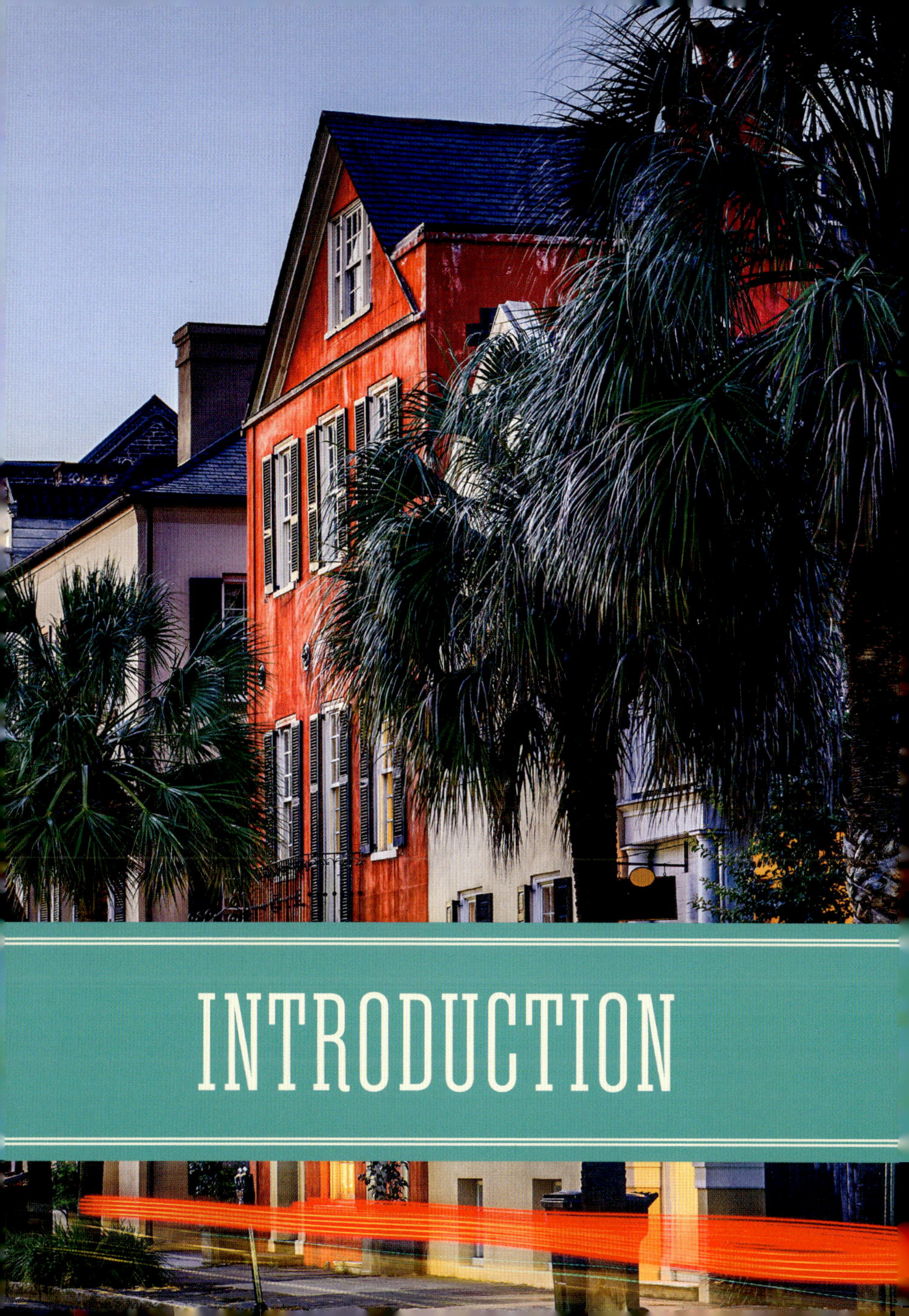

INTRODUCTION

A Brief History of Cocktails in South Carolina

Charleston, and thus South Carolina, was born in 1670. Planters had grown rich with Barbados's Caribbean sugar rush of the mid-1600s, and they were looking for a "next place" with steady timber supplies. What resulted is the transformation of the river delta landscape of the South Carolina Lowcountry into an indigo, rice, and cotton economy, surrounded by merchants and anchored by ports that reached a world far beyond them. Much of the blueprint that built the state was lifted from Barbados.

Charleston's waterfront, as depicted in 1762

"The historical connection between Barbados and Carolina is far deeper than a handful of influential colonists, or an architectural form, or a style of cuisine, or a dialect," says Dr. Nic Butler of the Charleston County Public Library and host of the *Charleston Time Machine* podcast. "Barbados, or more precisely the spirit of late seventeenth-century Barbados, was encoded in the DNA of Carolina from the moment this colony was conceived."

A British ship approaching Charleston. Painting by Thomas Leitch, ca. 1776.

With that culture came rum—and lots of it—traveling the well-sailed route from the Caribbean to Charleston, and the consumption of it transcended class, occupation, and sometimes race. Other spirits flowed through the port as well, including ciders, fortified wines like Madeira, exotic liqueurs from far-flung destinations, and even some gin from northern Europe, along with sugar, crates of citrus fruit and pineapples, and plenty of sugar.

As one of the oldest colonies in the Americas, South Carolina was at one time also one of the richest. Sure, Charleston had its share of houses of worship, but in a city where commerce often came first, public houses and taverns were much more common.

According to Paul Hibbard in "A History of South Carolina Liquor Regulation," South Carolina's first comprehensive liquor regulation was "AN ACT FOR REGULATING PUBLIQUE HOUSES," approved by the Lords Proprietors with the advice and consent of the General Assembly in January 1695. "The preamble took note of the 'unlimited number of Taverns, Tapp Houses, and Punch Houses, and the want of sobriety, honesty, and discretion in the owners or masters of such houses, [which] have and will encourage all such vices as usually are the productions of drunkenness.' The act prohibited the sale of any strong drink under the quantity of one gallon at a draught unless the seller obtained a license from then Governor Blake. Planters, however, could sell liquor on their own plantations."

The rivers were the "highways" of the time, and there was even a practice of selling liquor by boat to the plantations—a floating liquor store of sorts that would pull up at a plantation dock and leave much lighter in the cargo hold but heavier in the purse. However, enslaved persons were mostly prohibited from purchasing alcohol, no matter the location.

Beyond just the spirits, this state also had a high luxury for the time—ice. Butler says that "on April 7, 1817, the *Charleston City Gazette* noted the recent arrival of a brig from Boston (sixteen days' passage), carrying '200 tons [of] ice, for the Ice House lately established in this city.' From that moment in the spring of 1817 until the first shots of the American Civil War in April 1861, Charlestonians enjoyed a continuous supply of Yankee ice to cool our southern summers."

Charleston in ruins during the Civil War, as seen from the Circular Church, 150 Meeting Street

The Civil War Changes Everything

The Civil War changed life for all Americans, and most decidedly so for South Carolinians. Much of Columbia was burned, Charleston was occupied, and slavery was rightly abolished. However, the Black Codes of 1865 banned Black people from making or selling liquor. As the nineteenth century waxed on, Prohibition and its proponents began to shape the state, and their efforts are still having an effect to this day.

The South Carolina Dispensary system ran from 1892 until 1907. The state held a monopoly on all liquor sales, bottling liquor in palmetto-embossed bottles (highly collectible today), but the effort at control failed as a temperance movement and instead became a money-making machine that, even after it ceased as a statewide mandate in 1907, continued in some counties, with corruption running amok. The system was then abolished in 1915, when South Carolina adopted Prohibition five years earlier than the United States as a whole.

The Hell Hole Swamp, which prior to the war had been a prosperous rice-growing area in Berkeley County, became a hotbed of moonshining activity during the 1920s, with a direct pipeline of mason jars of moonshine making their way by boxcar to Al Capone in Chicago. Moonshine also was routinely delivered to Charleston residences, many of whom only barely felt the inconveniences of Prohibition. The swamp families had held their family moonshine recipes for generations, and soon competition turned into turf wars. In 1926, the Coast Guard sent a hundred federal agents via the *Yamacraw* to Charleston Harbor, and the next day, they raided the swamp. Close to thirty-five people were arrested in a two-day assault, and gallons of "the good stuff" were poured out on the sandy soil.

Blue Laws and Minis

Blue laws, aka Sunday laws, became the state norm—restricting sales of alcohol on Sunday, or altogether, in some counties, along with gambling or other "sinful" pursuits. To this day, the sale of liquor remains a county-by-county decision, though the house legislature did pass a bill in 2024 to allow liquor sales for limited hours on Sunday if the county wished to pursue it. At the time of this publication, you can get a Sunday drink in most bars and restaurants across the state, but liquor stores remain shuttered. There are no longer any dry counties in the state, but the state senate has yet to pass the bill for Sunday liquor-store sales.

One odd outcome of liquor regulation was the requirement that restaurants and bars mix drinks using mini bottles. After Federal Prohibition was lifted in 1933, South Carolina didn't simply go back to a free-for-all drinking environment. Patrons wishing to drink had to bring their own liquor—a practice called "brown bagging"—and the bar would charge for mixers and service. This became a popular practice, and then there was pushback to curtail that. Enter the mini bottle.

From 1973 to 2006—a much longer period than in other states—South Carolina bartenders did the best they could to keep the party going, and the distinctive sound of hundreds of little caps being cracked behind the bar all night became an ambient soundtrack for South Carolina's bars. Bargoers and bartenders created and shared a language of their own for ordering cocktails. Visit during this era, and you'd have to learn if you wanted "two shots, three ways" or, conversely, that some drinks would have to come in pitchers or be split, since staff had to use the bottles in full, which could be both overly strong and expensive. While it could be fun, it definitely hampered cocktail-crafting creativity.

Since the repeal in 2006 of the law requiring the use of mini bottles (though some old-school bartenders still can make "two shots, four ways"), craft cocktail culture has exploded in South Carolina. Bartenders increasingly use local ingredients and obscure liqueurs, and they find inspiration from larger craft cocktail cultures around the world.

Trends in South Carolina Cocktail Culture Today

The craft cocktail game is strongest in Charleston, a cultural leader of the state for more than four hundred years. Greenville is a strong runner-up, with the Midlands right behind, and although the Pee Dee and the Grand Strand have a way to go to embrace mixology methodology en masse, there are glimmers of good taste if you know where to look. However, these trends show up at the best places statewide:

1. **Fancy ice is a given.** Big cubes are standard, Swizzles routinely have pebble or crushed ice, and some spots, such as Seahorse in Charleston, have long, slender cubes that elegantly cool a highball glass.
2. **Fresh juice isn't just made from citrus.** From celery to bell pepper and blueberry, fresh juices are contributing Technicolor hues to many craft cocktails, even as they connect to the flavors of their regions.
3. **The carbonation quench is king.** Forced carbonation of cocktail elements, or whole cocktails, is the favorite party trick of some of the state's best bartenders. Much of South Carolina is hot and humid, and those crispy carbonation bubbles can quench like little else can when the temperature rises.
4. **Bourbon is nonnegotiable.** Bourbon is by far the most popular spirit in the state, and almost all craft cocktail joints have a version of the Old Fashioned, but for many, the nation's official spirit is a muse of sorts.
5. **Pears over peaches.** Pears are not really grown that much in the state, whereas South Carolina produces more peaches than Georgia. However, pear flavors show up all over the state's cocktail menus. South Carolina bartenders have embraced the pear vodka trend for fruity cocktails, and seem to be using pear much more than fresh peaches or peach-flavored spirits.

6. **Smoke is still in the air.** The smoked-cocktail trend is still popular in the state, though mainly outside of Charleston and Greenville.
7. **We're all fat-washing now.** Fat-washing, the technique of mixing a fat such as butter, animal fat, or olive oil with a liquor, is becoming a standard technique to add a silkier mouthfeel to cocktails statewide.
8. **Subtle garnishes are the move.** By far, the most popular garnish in South Carolina is the dehydrated orange wheel. Bartenders love it for its shelf stability and visual appeal, but it adds just a little to the cocktail flavor—unlike a lemon twist, for instance.

Bourbon: A New Foundation for Creativity

Bourbon is, by all accounts, South Carolina's favorite spirit. But why does this corn-based distilled liquor have such a firm grip on the state's cocktail-loving heart? Seán S. McKeithan provides a clue in his 2012 *Southern Cultures* essay entitled "Every Ounce a Man's Whiskey? Bourbon in the White Masculine South":

> The story of Bourbon's ascent from the ripe ground of the southern colonies into the collective consciousness of today's South is a story of thirst, industriousness, and, perhaps above all, corn. . . . By the late 1790s, a significant population of Scots-Irish had settled in Maryland and Southwest Pennsylvania and had "brought with them the strongly held opinion that whiskey, not bread, was the staff of life, the equipment for distilling, and an expert knowledge of the distiller's art." These settlers quickly took to squeezing liquor out of the land, using primarily local rye, but also grains,

> fruits, and even vegetables, distilling just about anything that could be made to ferment. As these settlers moved South through Appalachia to Kentucky across the Cumberland Gap, they discovered southern corn, the region's supercrop.

Beyond the facts of farming and immigration, bourbon became a way for Southern white men to express masculinity and reinforce it, McKeithan asserts. But these days, bourbon has outgrown its good ol' boys stereotype of yore. Distillers such as Charleston's High Wire Distilling Co. are using it to shore up South Carolina farming and tell new stories through old grain varieties—with delicious results. And the state's craft cocktailers are pushing bourbon's possibilities way beyond the Old Fashioned into new territory. As an example, see what Andy Rhine does in his clarified cocktail at Mr. Crisp in Greenville (see the recipe on page 244). In the South Carolina of today, bourbon has become a new foundation for creativity, even as it remains connected to its long, storied traditions.

Lane Becker

Building Your South Carolina Home Bar

Lane Becker is an important player in Charleston's quest for craft cocktail excellence. He tended bar at McCrady's and The Ordinary, helped open Babas and Last Saint, and is currently overseeing Basic Projects' beautiful and approachable bar programs at Post House and Sullivan's. Known among his peers for his level of cocktail sophistication, paired with a dry sense of humor and a truly welcoming personality behind the bar, he also has lots of thoughts about home bartending. Here he is in his own words.

LANE BECKER: When I first started working in fancy kitchens and bars, there was this tendency for me to be real snooty about everything. It was exhausting to my family and friends, when the whole point is to be together with your family and friends and make them something delicious and enjoyable.

My parents were always really good at throwing a party, and their thing was, "As long as somebody's staying, we're going to open another bottle if that's what people want to do." They were always generous about it, and that's always been important to me. I don't want to sweat when it's time to make another round of drinks; you can batch stuff ahead of time, or have some good, solid recipes that aren't sixteen minutes of shaking an egg white while people wait. Then you can have fun. Here's what I suggest for setting up your home bar.

GOOD-QUALITY WORKHORSE SPIRITS. Have all your favorite fancy things, sure, but you need some things that aren't precious and are mixable. Think a little bit like a commercial bar or restaurant bartender and come up with your well of good but affordable spirits—no plastic handles of things, but a good London dry gin, a vodka, a tequila, multiple rums because they are so handy here and I love them, and, of course, a good bourbon. That way you won't end up mixing up your favorite or special celebratory spirit for someone who "doesn't get it" and then being resentful about it. Resentment bartending isn't good hospitality.

Big ice mold, Lewis ice bag. Having molds for big ice is nice. Everyone likes a big ice cube, and it's cheap and always impresses people. But the best thing is starting with the regular ice that comes out of the freezer door and then using a Lewis bag to make crushed ice whenever you want. It's a cool showpiece for something like a Julep, and it's easy to store away when you're not using it.

Carbonator. A carbonator like a SodaStream is always helpful, and in Charleston I recommend as much fizzy stuff as possible. It makes everything more refreshing, and carbonating drinks or elements of drinks can up the flavor and quality possibilities. No one wants the dreaded flat tonic.

Cocktail tin shaker, long barspoon, Hawthorne strainer. These are standard, and they will get you very far.

Rocks glasses. The workhorses of bar glasses, so start here when it comes to glassware. From there, highball glasses and Nick & Noras are nice.

Punch bowl. Did I mention this makes it so fun? This can be the star element of your home craft cocktails, and it's a Charleston tradition.

Your SC Bar Shopping List

BITTERMILK, TIPPLEMAN'S. Joe and MariElena Raya have been a part of Charleston hospitality for years, but it was their time as founders of The Gin Joint, Charleston's first proper craft cocktail bar, that set them on their path. The Rayas handcrafted many of the syrups used in drinks served at the petite bar, and they began to realize, with limited space and equipment, what a challenge that was. So Bittermilk—a line of handcrafted cocktail mixers—was born, and then Tippleman's, the Rayas' craft cocktail syrups brand. It's all made in North Charleston. Ranging from Charred Grapefruit Tonic with Bulls Bay Sea Salt to Barrel Aged Cola Syrup, these highly crafted concoctions are a cut above the rest.

BLENHEIM GINGER ALE. There are ginger beers, and then there is Blenheim. Currently the oldest continuously independent soda bottler in the world, Blenheim created its Ginger Ale in the 1800s from a natural spring in Blenheim, in the Pee Dee's Marlboro County. The original bottling plant opened in 1903, and ninety years later, the company was purchased by the Schafer family, owners of the most famous tourist attraction in the Pee Dee, South of the Border. They renovated the original plant in Blenheim to meet new quality standards, and began bottling this unique ginger ale. Today, Blenheim has a new plant with a modern bottling system and more capacity at South of the Border, where Blenheim Ginger Ale is still produced today. It has a cult following among South Carolina bartenders, but if you see the famous "red cap," just know that this ginger ale comes with a serious kick.

HIGH WIRE DISTILLING CO. Charleston-based High Wire is most famous for its Jimmy Red Straight Bourbon Whiskey, which definitely needs a place on your cocktail cart. However, don't sleep on the Hat Trick Gin, which you'll see in recipes throughout this book.

Preparations and Techniques for the Home Bartender

Simple Syrup: Simple Syrup is simple. It's equal parts water and sugar, and in craft cocktails, that sugar is often (but not always) demerara sugar. Add equal parts water and sugar to a saucepot, bring the mixture to a simmer, and stir until the sugar is dissolved. Cool and bottle the syrup, then keep it in the refrigerator for 1 to 3 weeks. To make Rich Simple Syrup, double the amount of sugar. To make Demerara Syrup, substitute demerara sugar for white sugar.

Honey Syrup: Combine 2 parts honey to 1 part hot water and stir until the honey is dissolved, then bottle and store the syrup in the refrigerator for 1 to 3 weeks.

Saline Solution: Combine 20 grams salt with 80 grams hot distilled water and mix until the salt is dissolved. Allow the solution to cool, then place it in a bitters bottle to dispense via eyedropper. That's a 20% solution; to make a 10% solution, use 10 grams salt and 90 grams hot distilled water.

Dehydrated Citrus Garnishes: Preheat the oven to 200°F. Line a sheet tray with parchment paper, slice your citrus fruit into ¼-inch wheels, and place the wheels flat on the tray, making sure that none of the wheels are touching. Bake for 2 to 3 hours, checking often, until the citrus wheels are completely dehydrated. Allow the citrus wheels to cool and store them in an airtight container.

Shake: Add ice and your cocktail ingredients to a cocktail tin or shaker, fit the two pieces together snugly, and then shake for at least 15 seconds to cool, aerate, mix, and slightly dilute the ingredients.

DRY SHAKE: This technique—which is similar to the previously mentioned shake method, except that ice is not added to the tin—is used to create a froth from egg whites, aquafaba, or off-the-shelf foamers.

STRAIN: Separate the parts of the tin, then place a Hawthorne strainer over the mouth of the tin before pouring the contents of the tin into a glass. The Hawthorne strainer will catch any ice and large ingredient debris, resulting in a clearer cocktail that doesn't dilute so fast.

FINE STRAIN: In addition to using a Hawthorne strainer over the mouth of the tin, use a fine-mesh strainer over your glass, so that the cocktail is poured through both strainers on its way to the glass.

DOUBLE STRAIN: Place a small mesh strainer over a glass, and then strain as aforementioned.

LOWCOUNTRY

Charleston Light Dragoon's Punch
Black Manhattan
Huskwell Negroni
T'amaro Not Today
As You Wish
Pho Cocktail
Lowcountry Lemonade
Double Standard
Mash Old Fashioned
Red Wedding
Southern Gold
The Dirty Green Tomato
Chartreuse Swizzle
Bourbon Punch
Toki-O Drifting
Panic Button
Green Arrow
Cavalletta Cafe
Pink Cactus Margarita
Tavern Martini
Old Salt
Spaghettini
Bee's Sneeze
The Ambiguous Bird
Chiapas Paloma
Tropical Negroni

Rapsody
Moe's Bloody Mary
Mount Sage
Rosa Mexicana
Good Old Fashioned DP
Whatever You Say, Stove
Aged Eggnog
Spa Day
Sorrento Sun
Metadetector
Black Magic Woman
Gator Bite
Melon Ball
Gamechanger
Spice Girl
Pukalani Punch
Benne Goodman
Habersham Peach
Cathead Cooler
Summer's End
Blood Orange Gin Rickey
Lowcountry Oyster Shooter
Harvest Moon
Peachy Keen Mule

Charleston and the surrounding Lowcountry are the undisputed epicenter of both the culinary and craft cocktail landscape in South Carolina. In fact, Charleston, founded in 1670 and at one time one of the richest cities in the world due to rice production through enslaved labor, has been a driver of this continent's culture since at least the mid-1700s. Its busy port also brought people and goods from around the globe into the country, so the flavors and the spirits available—from rum to pineapple to spice blends from the trade routes of Asia—really informed drinking culture from the beginning.

Charleston's cocktail history is a long one. It started with punches concocted to celebrate some of the nation's first presidents, and continues to its present-day focus on craft with that same "global port" aesthetic when it comes to spirits and techniques. Add in the recent influence of culinary programs that emphasize the Lowcountry's bounty of ingredients, from citrus to celery and a growing number of local spirits, and it's easy to find a well-crafted cocktail in Charleston.

Get out of the city and into towns such as Beaufort or Georgetown and the pace and high precision might slow down, like the tidal creeks that often wind to the horizon, but Charleston's scene still influences, the most visual evidence of that being the focus on local ingredients.

CHARLESTON LIGHT DRAGOON'S PUNCH

HUSK
76 QUEEN STREET, CHARLESTON

A recipe from 1792 discovered in the Preservation Society of Charleston's archives, this cocktail recalls the best of the tea punches of that era; its revival has become ubiquitous with this Charleston restaurant. The Bar at Husk is actually a separate, adjacent building, all dark woods and low ceilings in the first-floor bar (with additional seating on the second floor), so sipping this cocktail in that environment only furthers the time-warp effect, at least until the bartenders use a computer to swipe your credit card for the bill.

GLASSWARE: Highball glass
GARNISH: Lemon peel

- **1¼ oz. Black Tea Syrup (see recipe)**
- **1 oz. brandy**
- **1 oz. Jamaican dark rum**
- **¾ oz. fresh lemon juice**
- **½ oz. peach brandy**
- **Club soda, to top**

1. Combine all of the ingredients, except for the club soda, in a cocktail shaker with ice and shake.
2. Strain the cocktail into a highball glass and top with club soda.
3. Garnish with a lemon peel.

Black Tea Syrup: In a saucepan over medium heat, combine 4 cups freshly brewed black tea and 2 cups raw sugar. Stir until the sugar is dissolved, then remove the mixture from heat and store it in a covered container or bottle. The syrup will keep for up to 1 week in the refrigerator.

HIGH WIRE DISTILLING CO.

"Everything we do begins with a quest for flavor," says Scott Blackwell, cofounder, along with his wife, Ann Marshall, of High Wire Distilling Co. in Charleston. And since 2013, that pursuit has led them to create a bevy of distinctive spirits, from a botanical gin and watermelon brandy to a bourbon that is fueling a seismic shift in the American bourbon market.

It all began when they decided to focus on grain as the most important building block in their spirits, as opposed to water, filtration, or barrels. Since bourbon is by law 51 percent corn, corn was where they began, searching for a varietal that would both express the terroir of South Carolina and also taste distinctively delicious.

"That led us to Glenn Roberts of Anson Mills," Marshall says, "and he introduced us to Jimmy Red corn, an old bootlegger's corn that had been passed down on James Island through generations." However, when the couple decided that yes, that was their corn, there was one major problem.

There wasn't enough of the corn to distill. In fact, there were barely six ears left in existence.

Nevertheless, instead of looking elsewhere, the two chose the hard path, deciding to grow out Jimmy Red for a couple of seasons—in partnership with Clemson University Cooperative Extension—in order to get enough grain to distill. Blackwell is a Culinary Institute of America–trained baker, and they just had a hunch this one was special.

Boy, were they right. More than a decade later, High Wire Distilling Co.'s Jimmy Red Straight Bourbon Whiskey is racking up the accolades, from a Double Gold at the 2025 San Francisco World Spirits Competition to a feature and the cover photo in *Whiskey Advocate*, April 2025. What makes it so delicious is the corn, which is 100 percent of the mash bill. However, because of the corn, it's a highly nuanced spirit, with various flavors that read from graham cracker to vanilla, and a high corn-oil content, which delivers a creamy finish.

This focus on South Carolina products and producers now extends throughout the distilling program, from rye to single-farm peaches for the peach brandy. In 2024, High Wire purchased 6,400 tons of grain from South Carolina farmers, a real impact on agriculture in the state. And Jimmy Red is back in commercial production, grown by both High Wire's contracted farmers and beyond. Now it's even available as grits.

The distillery has expanded too, moving from its original 6,500-square-foot location to a 23,000-square-foot facility on Huger Street in a beautifully preserved warehouse. Its main attraction is the 8,000-liter custom-built CARL still from Germany, which has increased production immensely, allowing High Wire to expand. But in the end, Marshall says, the farm is always the foundation for what they do, which they illustrate with this oft-repeated phrase: "Drinking is an agricultural act."

BLACK MANHATTAN

THE BAR AT HIGH WIRE DISTILLING CO.
311 HUGER STREET, CHARLESTON

High Wire Distilling Co.'s owners, Ann Marshall and Scott Blackwell, have roots in farming and organic baking, and since opening the distillery in 2013, they have quietly revolutionized not only the spirits world but also South Carolina agriculture through focusing on reclaiming flavors and grains that have previously been lost or forgotten. From Jimmy Red Straight Bourbon Whiskey that helped bring the almost-extinct Jimmy Red corn back into commercial production to Abruzzi Rye Whiskey, featured here, their spirits are expressions of South Carolina terroir with every sip.

GLASSWARE: **Nick & Nora glass**
GARNISH: **Bourbon cherry, lemon peel**

- **2 oz. High Wire Distilling Co. Abruzzi Rye Whiskey**
- **¾ oz. High Wire Distilling Co. Southern Amaro**
- **¼ oz. Luxardo Maraschino Originale**
- **Dash Regans' Orange Bitters No. 6**
- **Dash Angostura bitters**

1. Chill a Nick & Nora glass. Combine all of the ingredients in a mixing glass, add ice, and stir.
2. Strain the cocktail into the chilled Nick & Nora and garnish with a bourbon cherry and lemon peel.

HUSKWELL NEGRONI

ESTADIO
122 SPRING STREET, CHARLESTON

Estadio is a Spanish tapas restaurant with a decidedly Southern accent, so naturally, *Gintonics* might typically be the go-to move here. However, since they use (wholesale-only) Sweatman's tonic, they aren't replicable at home. This Negroni, which also features a locally made ingredient, is. Huskwell Cascara, a loose-tea-like product made from the outer husks of coffee berries, is available for retail purchase, and when infused in a dry gin, it lends notes of hibiscus, dried fruits, and molasses to the classic three-part cocktail.

GLASSWARE: Rocks glass
GARNISH: Lemon peel

- **1 oz. Cascara-Infused Gin (see recipe)**
- **1 oz. Atxa Red Vermouth**
- **1 oz. Campari**

1. Combine all of the ingredients in a cocktail shaker with ice and shake thoroughly.
2. Strain the cocktail into a rocks glass over a large ice cube, then garnish with a lemon peel.

CASCARA-INFUSED GIN: Add 200 grams Huskwell Cascara to 1 (1 liter) bottle of Beefeater Gin and steep for at least 1 week before use. Strain and rebottle.

DOAR BROS.

Some of the best cocktail bars feel akin to jewel boxes lined in plush velvet. In the case of Doar Bros. on Meeting Street, Charleston, that velvet is a lush shade of navy blue, enveloping the small space in after-dusk tones that feel luxurious. It's an evident contrast to its location, a well-worn block of the city where, depending on the time of day, hawkers may be trying to entice passersby with free hush puppies, or large groups may be headed to the Charleston City Market, in eyesight from the bar's front door. However, step inside Doar Bros. and the air changes, becoming more relaxed and inviting.

The name isn't a mirage—it really is a family affair at Doar Bros., where Adam Doar is general manager and his brother, Jonathan, is the chef behind the scenes, plating nightly caviar service, marinated mussels, brown butter popcorn, or on special Wednesdays at least once a quarter, courses of Italian dishes for a full-blown dinner experience. Jonathan's wife, Marinela Vicente Doar, is responsible for the interior design and decor.

The cocktails are listed in two categories: modern, seasonal cocktails that show off the staff's creativity, and classics, "for those who want what they want," Jonathan says. "Sometimes new guests are the most rewarded in the sense that we can offer new knowledge to their palate. Honestly, we are able and excited to accommodate anyone who walks through those doors."

The main focus of Doar Bros. is simply consistent excellence, which encompasses balanced cocktails that are interesting and innovative while still being approachable, solid execution of those cocktails no matter who is behind the bar, and a relaxed hospitality that begins with the owners and often feels more like a lovely living-room experience at a friend's house than a bustling bar on a Saturday night.

"It's amazing to be able to work with my brother," says Jonathan. "The fact that we are able to live this dream together is amazing and something that we can look back on when we're old and just appreciate this time we had together in the trenches."

DOAR
BROS.
DOAR BROS.

T'AMARO NOT TODAY

DOAR BROS.
225 MEETING STREET, CHARLESTON

Doar Bros. is not only a beautiful jewel box of a bar, it's also consistently excellent, despite an ever-rotating assortment of drinks. Take this cocktail, for instance, created by bartender Xander Peters. Cachaça, a Brazilian spirit that is made with fermented sugarcane, usually stays on the tropical beaches, but here it takes a Daiquiri-style detour to the Italian alps. This drink is akin to wearing tropical perfume in the brisk mountain air: funky, herbaceous, and slightly minty, but with a depth that hints at future summer days. An added bonus? It's easy to make.

GLASSWARE: **Coupe glass**

- **1 oz. Braulio Amaro**
- **1 oz. fresh lime juice**
- **¾ oz. Simple Syrup (see recipe on page 20)**
- **½ oz. Novo Fogo Silver Cachaça**

1. Combine all of the ingredients in a cocktail shaker filled with ice and shake until nice and frothy.
2. Strain the cocktail into a coupe.

AS YOU WISH

BABAS ON CANNON
11 CANNON STREET, CHARLESTON

This cocktail is a Babas classic, introduced on the opening menu and inspired by the fresh pomegranate juice stands that fill the autumn streets of Istanbul. It was originally designed as a pomegranate Margarita, but because the staff accidentally omitted tequila on the opening-night liquor order, they constructed it with gin instead, then rum, then multiple other spirits, finding it was delicious every time. The name is a fitting homage to Westley's repeated line in *The Princess Bride*, the only book in the restaurant for its opening year. Adding a large slice of citrus peel in the shaker with the ice and other ingredients is termed a "regal shake." During shaking, the ice helps express the oils and bitterness from the peel, lending an elegant note to the finished cocktail.

GLASSWARE: Highball glass

- **1½ oz. spirit of your choice**
- **1½ oz. fresh pomegranate juice**
- **¾ oz. Demerara Syrup (see recipe on page 20)**
- **¾ oz. fresh lemon juice**
- **⅛ oz. Campari**
- **Orange peel**

1. Combine all of the ingredients, including the orange peel, in a cocktail shaker with ice and shake.
2. Strain the cocktail into a highball glass with four large ice cubes.

Pho Spice Syrup: Heat a medium saucepan over medium heat and add 1 cup water, 1 cup sugar, 10 star anise pods, 2 cinnamon sticks, and 5 cloves, stirring to incorporate. Continue simmering, stirring often, for 10 minutes, until the sugar is dissolved. Cool the syrup and place it in a bottle or closed container without straining. This will keep for 7 to 10 days in the refrigerator.

PHO COCKTAIL

PINK BELLIES
595 KING STREET, SUITE 1, CHARLESTON

Chef Thai Phi started Pink Bellies as a food truck, but his King Street location is a highly designed space with a West Coast vibe and a "cool kids" atmosphere to match, especially on the weekends. However, the food (and cocktails) have as much homemade heart as they always did. Pho, the well-known Vietnamese dish of broth, rice noodles, herbs, and meat or tofu, is obviously the inspiration for this drink. However, this is not simply a party trick or caricature—the cocktail is delicious on its own and serves up a hefty dose of savory umami.

GLASSWARE: **Coupe glass**

GARNISH: **Lime wheel, star anise**

- **2 oz. gin**
- **¾ oz. Pho Spice Syrup (see recipe)**
- **¾ oz. fresh lime juice**
- **Dash fish sauce**
- **Dash sriracha**
- **3 to 4 dashes orange bitters**

1. Combine all of the ingredients in a cocktail shaker with ice and shake.
2. Strain the cocktail into a coupe and garnish with a lime wheel and star anise.

LOWCOUNTRY LEMONADE

FIREFLY DISTILLERY
4201 SPRUILL AVENUE, NORTH CHARLESTON

In 2008, Charleston County's Firefly Distillery introduced its Sweet Tea Vodka to the market, inspired by the only tea plantation in North America, located on Wadmalaw Island. To say that this black tea–infused spirit with a dose of sweetness was a hit is an understatement; within nine months, Firefly Sweet Tea Vodka was distributed in all fifty states, and this cocktail—a grown-up version of the Arnold Palmer—has become a new South Carolina classic at bars and golf courses, and everywhere in between. It's easy to make and easy drinking, and it still quenches the thirst when the humidity gets high.

GLASSWARE: **Rocks glass or jelly jar**
GARNISH: **Lemon slice**

- **1½ oz. Firefly Sweet Tea Vodka**
- **3 oz. lemonade**

1. Pour the vodka and lemonade into a rocks glass or jelly jar filled with ice. Stir with a barspoon to combine.
2. Garnish with a lemon slice.

DOUBLE STANDARD

THE COCKTAIL CLUB
479 KING STREET, CHARLESTON

With more than a decade on Upper King, The Cocktail Club seems to be a solid staple in Charleston, but it once felt like a secret, with its simple dark door and rooms of crumbling fireplace mantels and Charleston architecture ghosts. In fact, it looks much like what Indigo Road Hospitality Group founder Steve Palmer saw when he first peeked through a hole in the ceiling of the restaurant downstairs—rooms straddling space and time—and he said, "We need to leave this alone and build a bar." And so it stands, and this cocktail with it.

GLASSWARE: **Coupe glass**
GARNISH: **Jalapeño slice, cilantro leaf**

- **¾ oz. Ginger Syrup (see recipe)**
- **½ oz. fresh lime juice**
- **4 sprigs cilantro**
- **2 serrano peppers**
- **1 oz. Cucumber-Infused Vodka (see recipe)**
- **1 oz. Serrano-Infused Gin (see recipe)**
- **2 dashes celery bitters**

1. In a cocktail shaker, muddle the Ginger Syrup, lime juice, cilantro, and serranos.
2. Add ice, the spirits, and the bitters.
3. Shake, double strain the cocktail into a coupe, and then garnish with a slice of jalapeño and a cilantro leaf.

Ginger Syrup: Combine 1 cup sugar, 1 cup water, and ¼ pound ginger, pulverized in a blender, in a medium pot over medium heat. Stir until the sugar is dissolved and the syrup begins to simmer. Remove it from heat and allow the syrup to steep for 15 minutes, then double strain and cool. The syrup will keep for 1 month in the refrigerator.

Cucumber-Infused Vodka: Combine 2 English cucumbers, peeled and roughly chopped, with 1 liter vodka in a bowl or container. Let the vodka infuse for 24 to 48 hours, then strain and rebottle.

Serrano-Infused Gin: Combine 1½ to 2 serrano peppers, sliced, and 1 liter gin in a bowl or container. Let the gin infuse for 24 to 48 hours, then strain and rebottle.

MASH OLD FASHIONED

BAR MASH
701 EAST BAY STREET, CHARLESTON

Bar Mash is an American whiskey and beer bar located in the Cigar Factory complex on East Bay Street, and the low ceilings, dark wood, and bottles of bourbon behind the bar all fit the theme. Thus it makes sense that this is a place to come to for an Old Fashioned, and Mash's version utilizes a subtle twist—gomme (gum) syrup.

GLASSWARE: Rocks glass
GARNISH: Orange peel

- **2 oz. Elijah Craig Small Batch**
- **¼ oz. Monin Gum Syrup**
- **Dash Angostura bitters**
- **Dash Bittermens Hopped Grapefruit Bitters**

1. Combine all of the ingredients in a cocktail glass with ice and stir until chilled.
2. Strain the cocktail into a rocks glass with a large ice cube and garnish with an orange peel.

RED WEDDING

EDMUND'S OAST
1081 MORRISON DRIVE, CHARLESTON

Edmund's Oast has been a destination on Morrison Drive since its opening day on Valentine's Day 2014, and this cocktail has been a constant on the menu from that moment. The genius of this drink is that it subtly changes flavor and composition as the ice melts, making each sip a delicious new experience. The earthy flavor of hibiscus and black tea is the spine of this drink, so avoid cutting corners and attempting to make the cubes out of a pre-made hibiscus punch—it won't yield the same results.

GLASSWARE: **Rocks glass**

- **Orange peel**
- **½ oz. Amaro Averna**
- **3 Hibiscus Ice Cubes (see recipe)**
- **2 oz. Maker's Mark**

1. In a rocks glass, muddle the orange peel with the Averna.
2. Add the Hibiscus Ice Cubes, top with the bourbon, and give the cocktail a small stir.

Hibiscus Ice Cubes: In a container, combine 2 cups demerara sugar, 1½ cups dried hibiscus, ½ cup loose-leaf black tea, 1 (12 oz.) bottle of ginger beer, and a small bunch of thyme and top with 6 cups hot water. Stir until the sugar is dissolved. Let the tea steep overnight in the refrigerator, then strain out the solids. Add the liquid to silicone ice molds and freeze, for approximately 4 to 6 hours, until solid.

SOUTHERN GOLD

THE GIN JOINT
182 EAST BAY STREET #2169, CHARLESTON

The Gin Joint was one of the first cocktail bars to open in the city in 2010, and through ownership changes and a shifting cityscape in the last fifteen years, it still operates at a high-craft level. James Bolt and his team primarily have a culinary background, and "we really love to use the bounty of produce and ingredients that the Lowcountry has to offer," Bolt says, including the Carolina Gold rice that made Charleston wealthy. It's a natural pairing with other in-season ingredients they source, such as bell peppers, which here lend a fresh vibrancy to bitter Suze.

GLASSWARE: Rocks glass

GARNISH: Bay leaf

- 2 oz. Carolina Gold Rice Orgeat (see recipe)
- 1½ oz. Barr Hill Gin
- ¾ oz. fresh lemon juice
- ¾ oz. Simple Syrup (see recipe on page 20)
- ½ oz. Bell Pepper–Infused Suze (see recipe)
- ½ oz. Don Ciccio & Figli Finocchietto
- 2 dashes Creole bitters

1. Combine all of the ingredients in a cocktail shaker filled with ice and shake hard for 15 to 20 seconds.
2. Double strain the cocktail into a rocks glass, top with crushed ice, and garnish with a bay leaf.

Carolina Gold Rice Orgeat: Preheat the oven to 350°F. Place 5 oz. Carolina Gold rice on a baking sheet and toast for 10 to 15 minutes, until slightly brown. In a saucepan over medium heat, add the toasted rice, 2 bay leaves, and 24 oz. plain rice milk and simmer over a low flame for 15 to 20 minutes, until the rice has become somewhat tender. Add 1½ cups sugar, 1 cup water, and ¼ teaspoon salt and continue to cook on low for 5 to 7 minutes, until the sugar is dissolved. Drain the rice into a chinois, and catch all the rice liquid, blend reserve it. Remove the bay leaves. Add half of the rice back to the reserved rice liquid and blend on medium speed for 30 to 45 seconds, and then strain. This will keep for 5 to 7 days in the refrigerator.

Bell Pepper–Infused Suze: Add 1 (750 ml) bottle of Suze L'Originale and 1 yellow bell pepper, chopped and seeds removed, to a blender and blend on high for 45 to 50 seconds. Strain the infusion through cheesecloth and rebottle.

Green Tomato Pickle: Place a large canning pot on the stove and fill it with enough water to cover jars. In a pan over medium heat, toast 3 tablespoons mustard seeds, 2 tablespoons black peppercorns, and 2 tablespoons celery seeds until fragrant, then remove the seeds from heat and set aside. In a large bowl, combine 1 onion, julienned; 3 pounds green tomatoes, sliced into ¼-inch slices; and 3 jalapeños, thinly sliced, and then pack them into sterilized jars. Divide the toasted spices between the jars. Heat the canning pot to boiling. In a separate pot, bring 5 cups white vinegar, 2½ cups sugar, and 2 teaspoons salt to a boil, then turn off the heat. Carefully pour the vinegar mixture into the jars, leaving about ¼ inch of headroom at the top of the jars. Seal the jars but not too snugly. Place the sealed jars in the boiling water, let the water return to a boil, and boil for 10 minutes. Carefully remove the jars, let them rest on a cooling rack or tea towels for about 15 minutes, and then invert the jars for several hours to ensure the seal is complete.

THE DIRTY GREEN TOMATO

THE GROCERY
4 CANNON STREET, CHARLESTON

This cocktail made its debut when The Grocery first opened in 2011, because executive chef Kevin Johnson wanted a Dirty Martini with a more diverse flavor profile beyond that of just olive brine. "The pickled green tomato juice that we had on hand provided that, and it was a great way to further use product, something that's always been part of our ethos," he says. Now, during certain times of the year, the kitchen finds itself producing pickled tomatoes just to keep up with demand for this cocktail, which is a compelling combination of sour brine and botanical-forward gin.

GLASSWARE: **Coupe glass**

GARNISH: **Skewered quarter of a Green Tomato Pickle (see recipe)**

- **2¼ oz. High Wire Distilling Co. Hat Trick Gin**
- **1¼ oz. Green Tomato Pickle (see recipe) brine**

1. Chill a coupe glass. Combine the gin and pickle brine in a cocktail shaker with ice and shake vigorously for 10 to 15 seconds to aerate and get the liquid icy cold.
2. Strain the cocktail into the chilled coupe and garnish with a skewered quarter of a Green Tomato Pickle.

CHARTREUSE SWIZZLE

MAISON
708 KING STREET, CHARLESTON

Chartreuse is a storied spirit, created by Carthusian monks in 1737 using a secret mixture of one hundred and thirty herbs and flowers. Both its origin story and its irreplaceable herbal flavor make it a favorite among bartenders. At Maison, partner Will Love creates his version of this modern classic from San Francisco, using (among other ingredients) a sugarcane rum to bring out vegetal flavors. Although it isn't currently on the restaurant's menu due to a Chartreuse shortage, it's true refreshment with a French accent for Charleston heat and humidity.

GLASSWARE: **Highball glass**
GARNISH: **Lime wheel**

- **1 oz. pineapple juice**
- **¾ oz. Green Chartreuse**
- **¾ oz. fresh lime juice**
- **½ oz. John D. Taylor's Velvet Falernum**
- **½ oz. Dolin Génépy le Chamois Liqueur**
- **¼ oz. Neisson Blanc Rhum Agricole**
- **10 dashes Angostura bitters**

1. Combine all of the ingredients, except for the bitters, in a cocktail shaker with ice and shake.
2. Strain the cocktail into a highball glass filled with crushed ice, add the bitters on top of the ice, and garnish with a lime wheel.

The
AMERICA
970 MORRISON
CHARLESTON
(843) 81-

BOURBON PUNCH

THE ROYAL AMERICAN
970 MORRISON DRIVE, CHARLESTON

Located with a train-track view on Morrison Drive, The Royal American not only is one of the best places to see live music in town, but it also has a can't-miss patty melt and loaded baked potatoes served until late, making it a local's go-to all around. In fact, check the cabinet of many a Charleston resident, and you're likely to see a Royal American white souvenir cup, which more than likely first held bourbon punch when it was received. This most beloved of the Royal American punches—there's also a rum version and a vodka version—is actually a variation on an Arnold Palmer, and co-owner John Kenney suspects that is why it's so popular. It's a true crowd-pleaser.

GLASSWARE: Punch bowl with cups
GARNISH: Lemon wedge, cherry

- 2¾ liters water
- 2 (750 ml) bottles bourbon
- 1½ cups sugar
- 9 oz. frozen orange juice concentrate
- 8 oz. Luzianne Sweetened Iced Tea Concentrate
- 6 oz. frozen lemonade concentrate
- 2 oz. fresh lemon juice

1. Combine all of the ingredients in a punch bowl or other serving vessel and stir well.
2. Serve the punch over ice and garnish with a lemon wedge and cherry.

TOKI-O DRIFTING

O-KU
463 KING STREET, CHARLESTON

A sushi bar by evening that shifts to a distinct lounge vibe as the night wears on, O-Ku on Upper King has always been known for its creative cocktailing and a staff that enjoys high energy. One of their favorite tunes to keep the night moving and the party going is "Tokyo Drifting" by Glass Animals with Denzel Curry. This cocktail is a play on the song title and the unique Japanese racing style.

GLASSWARE: Rocks glass

GARNISH: Dehydrated orange wheel

- **1½ oz. Suntory Whisky Toki**
- **1 oz. Spiced Tea Syrup (see recipe)**
- **½ oz. Cynar**
- **½ oz. yuzu juice**
- **5 dashes Bittermens 'Elemakule Tiki Bitters**

1. Combine all of the ingredients in a cocktail tin filled with ice and shake.
2. Strain the cocktail into a rocks glass with a big ice cube and garnish with a dehydrated orange wheel.

SPICED TEA SYRUP: Add 4 Celestial Seasonings Bengal Spice tea bags to 1 quart boiling water and allow them to steep for 15 to 20 minutes. Strain the tea into a pot with 1 quart sugar, return the syrup to a boil, and then reduce the heat and slowly simmer for 30 minutes. Remove the syrup from heat, cool it, and place it in an air-tight container.

PANIC BUTTON

THE LIVING ROOM AT THE DEWBERRY
334 MEETING STREET, CHARLESTON

Outfitted with mid-century furnishings, a curated reading library, and a showstopping brass bar, The Living Room at The Dewberry immediately became a locals' haunt as well as a visitor haven when it opened in 2016 in a former federal building adjacent to Marion Square. This cocktail, originally created by Ryan Casey and on the menu ever since, is boozy, tongue-in-cheek, and, with a little ice magic, a showstopper on its own.

GLASSWARE: Coupe glass

- **1½ oz. bourbon**
- **¾ oz. Amaro Averna**
- **½ oz. Campari**
- **½ oz. Heering Cherry Liqueur**
- **¼ oz. fresh lemon juice**
- **Lemon peel, for zesting**

1. Combine all of the ingredients, except for the lemon peel, in a cocktail shaker with ice and shake.
2. Strain the cocktail into a coupe filled with a large ice sphere, then zest a lemon over the top and discard the peel.

GREEN ARROW

FIG
232 MEETING STREET, CHARLESTON

A vibrantly hued beverage that evokes all the fresh green growth of spring is very on-brand for FIG, a lauded Charleston restaurant that celebrates Lowcountry farmers and fishermen through an ever-evolving menu. Although this recipe calls for two subrecipes, the time invested is worth the effort; both the Pea Cordial and the Ginger Base are easily frozen for future use, so, with just a little work, you'll be able to serve these beautiful, zippy, green beverages regardless of the season.

GLASSWARE: Highball glass
GARNISH: Celery stick, lime wheel

- **1½ oz. Gin Mare**
- **¾ oz. Pea Cordial (see recipe)**
- **½ oz. Dolin Blanc Vermouth**
- **½ oz. Salers Gentian Apéritif**
- **½ oz. fresh lime juice**
- **¼ oz. Saline Solution (see recipe on page 20)**
- **¼ oz. Ginger Base (see recipe)**
- **3 dashes Bittermens Orchard Street Celery Shrub**
- **1 oz. soda water, to top**

1. Combine all of the ingredients, except for the soda, in a cocktail shaker with ice and shake.
2. Strain the cocktail into a highball glass filled with ice.
3. Top with the soda and garnish with a celery stick and lime wheel.

PEA CORDIAL: Combine 92 grams English peas, blanched; 45 grams Rich Simple Syrup (see recipe on page 20); and 45 grams Ketel One Vodka in a blender and puree thoroughly until smooth. Stir in 182 grams sugar snap pea juice. Store the cordial in the refrigerator for up to 1 week or freeze in small portions for longer storage.

GINGER BASE: Mix 1 part freshly juiced ginger to 2 parts fresh lemon juice and 3 parts Simple Syrup (see recipe on page 20). (Add club soda to any extra ginger base, and it becomes proper ginger beer.)

CAVALLETTA CAFE

FACULTY LOUNGE
391 HUGER STREET, CHARLESTON

Ring the bell to enter the Faculty Lounge, and as soon as the door shuts behind you, you already feel cooler, and that's even before sipping a cocktail like this. A collaborative creative effort by Jorge Arroyo and Nate Kearton, it's an Espresso Martini–inspired riff on a Grasshopper that feels anything but tired, despite the fact that this trend shows no sign of slowing. "Instant coffee packs from nearby grocer H&L are one of our favorite secret ingredients—we always have them on hand for staff or guest pick-me-ups," says co-owner Nayda Hutson, "so it was only a matter of time before they found their way into a cocktail."

GLASSWARE: **Coupe glass**

- **1½ oz. Brugal Añejo Rum**
- **¾ oz. Brancamenta**
- **¾ oz. Tempus Fugit Spirits Crème de Cacao**
- **1 Maxim Original or Mocha Gold Mild instant coffee powder pack**
- **1 to 3 dashes Fee Brothers Fee Foam**

1. Combine all of the ingredients in a cocktail shaker and dry shake (without ice) vigorously for 30 seconds.
2. Add ice and shake for 30 more seconds. (Be sure to shake hard or the coffee granules won't dissolve, resulting in a grainy texture.)
3. Double strain the cocktail into a coupe.

PINK CACTUS MARGARITA

PINK CACTUS
100-A SPRING STREET, CHARLESTON

There is something about drinking a hot-pink-hued Margarita, as the sun slips below the houses in the Elliotborough-Cannonborough neighborhood, that just screams warm spring nights in the city. Pink Cactus uses San Antonio's Brushfire Farms Prickly Pear Simple Syrup for its superior quality and flavor, and black volcanic sea salt for the salty glass rim, a nod to Oaxaca and its black clay soil. It's not only visually stunning but also stunningly delicious.

GLASSWARE: Rocks glass
GARNISH: Lime wheel

- **¾ oz. fresh lime juice**
- **Black sea salt, for the rim**
- **1½ oz. Lunazul Tequila Blanco**
- **½ oz. Brushfire Farms Prickly Pear Simple Syrup**
- **¼ oz. Simple Syrup** **(see recipe on page 20)**

1. Wet the rim of a rocks glass with lime juice, then dip the rim in black sea salt to give the glass a rim.
2. Combine the remaining ingredients in a cocktail tin with ice and shake.
3. Strain the cocktail into the rimmed glass over fresh ice, then garnish with a lime wheel.

TAVERN MARTINI

LOWLAND
36 GEORGE STREET, CHARLESTON

It takes a lot of talent to play with a classic—and yes, one of THE classics in the cocktail canon—and still offer a new spin. The team at Lowland accomplishes this with a smart garnish of herb oil element to make the Martini feel fresh and new. It's very in step with the restaurant as a whole, where classics from burgers to fried quail feel current but comfortable, and make it easy to stay for another round. For the spirit, use Citadelle Original Gin or Ketel One Vodka.

GLASSWARE: **Nick & Nora glass**

GARNISH: **5 drops Herb Oil (see recipe), olive or pickle on a skewer**

- **2 oz. gin or vodka**
- **1 oz. Dolin Dry Vermouth**

1. Combine the spirit and vermouth in a mixing glass with ice and stir.
2. Strain the cocktail into a Nick & Nora, then garnish with the Herb Oil drops and a skewered pickle or olive.

HERB OIL: Bring a pot of water to a boil and prepare an ice bath. Add 1 cup parsley leaves, 1 cup tarragon leaves, 1 cup basil leaves, and 1 cup dill fronds to the boiling water and blanch for 20 seconds. Remove them from the water and immediately place them in the ice bath. Drain, squeezing out excess water, and then add the herbs to a blender with 1 cup extra-virgin olive oil and blend until smooth. Strain the mixture through cheesecloth and store it in a sealed container.

OLD SALT

LAST SAINT
472 MEETING STREET, CHARLESTON

Last Saint is that high-low vibe that Charleston loves: highly crafted cocktails with a dive-bar soul. Created by partners Brandon Bramhall and Zachary Pease, who both worked at Attaboy in NYC, and local Joey Goetz of Bar George (and The Belmont, back in the day), this drink is one of the constants on an always-evolving menu. A frothy, salty cousin to the Paloma, it's perhaps a better use for that milk frother you just knew you'd use with every morning coffee.

GLASSWARE: Highball glass
GARNISH: Grapefruit wedge, salted

- 4 oz. fresh grapefruit juice
- 1½ oz. blanco tequila
- ¾ oz. Simple Syrup (see recipe on page 20)
- ½ oz. fresh lime juice
- 3 dashes Saline Solution (see recipe on page 20)

1. Whip the grapefruit juice with a frother or in a blender until fluffy.
2. Combine the juice and the remaining ingredients in a cocktail shaker, but do not stir or shake.
3. Pour the cocktail into a highball glass filled with ice, and perch a salted grapefruit wedge at the top of the glass.

SPAGHETTINI

LEON'S OYSTER SHOP
698 KING STREET, CHARLESTON

On a sunny day, there's definitely going to be a wait at Leon's, because sitting on the patio, eating oysters and fried chicken, just about feels like heaven. Many of the lucky patrons will be sipping cocktails that include Jack Rudy tonic—proprietor Brooks Reitz created the brand—but if it's sultry, locals in the know might opt for a six-pack of Miller High Life Ponies, or this easy-drinking cocktail that uses them. It's a mini-me version of the Spaghett from Wet City Brewing in Baltimore.

GLASSWARE: **12-oz. glass**
GARNISH: **Lemon peel, expressed**

- **1 oz. Aperol**
- **¼ oz. fresh lemon juice**
- **Miller High Life Pony, to top**

1. Add the Aperol and lemon juice to a glass filled with ice.
2. Express a lemon peel over the drink, then add the peel as a garnish.
3. Add the beer until the drink reaches the top and serve any left in the bottle alongside the cocktail.

BEE'S SNEEZE

THE BAR AT THE SPECTATOR
67 STATE STREET, CHARLESTON

Allen Lancaster loved High Wire Distilling Co.'s Barrel Rested Gin so much that, years after they stopped producing it, he commissioned a single barrel bottling for The Bar at The Spectator. He has that kind of pull because he's been the head bartender at this hotel for almost a decade, holding court in the hotel's lobby through some classic cocktail magic. His subtle sorcery includes serving an updated Bee's Knees with a lavender-infused honey, accentuating Hat Trick's lavender-forward profile, while the barrel-aged aspect adds a basement floor of deeper flavor to the classic cocktail.

GLASSWARE: Martini glass
GARNISH: Edible flowers

- **2 oz. Hat Trick Barrel Rested Gin**
- **¾ oz. Lavender Honey (see recipe)**
- **¾ oz. fresh lemon juice**
- **1 egg white**
- **Spritz Perfume (see recipe)**

1. Combine all of the ingredients, except for the Spritz Perfume, in a cocktail shaker filled with ice and shake.
2. Strain the cocktail into a martini glass, spritz with the Spritz Perfume, and garnish with edible flowers.

Lavender Honey: Combine 1 cup water and 2 tablespoons dried lavender in a medium saucepan. Bring the mixture to a boil and immediately reduce the heat to a simmer. Simmer for 4 minutes. Add 1 cup honey and stir to incorporate. Pour the syrup contents through a fine-mesh strainer and allow it to cool uncovered. Store it in the refrigerator for 7 to 10 days.

Spritz Perfume: In an atomizer bottle, combine equal parts orange blossom water and rose water.

THE AMBIGUOUS BIRD

THE ARCHER
601 MEETING STREET, SUITE 140, CHARLESTON

Jimmy Chmielewski and Damien Eden's inspiration behind The Ambiguous Bird was to create a lighter, more refreshing rendition of a Jungle Bird, maintaining all of the funky tiki elements of the classic cocktail, but making it more approachable for those who shy away from bitter. "The two components that really make this drink pop for us is the use of the coconut milk oolong Campari and the forced carbonation," Chmielewski says. Campari is bitter, sure, but gets a hefty dose of floral from the infusion, and carbonating the concoction puts it in contention as a porch pounder. Use El Dorado 5 Year Old Rum or Ten To One Caribbean Dark Rum.

GLASSWARE: Highball glass
GARNISH: 3 pineapple leaves

- **1¾ oz. water**
- **1½ oz. demerara rum**
- **1¼ oz. pineapple juice**
- **½ oz. Toasted Coconut and Oolong Tea Campari (see recipe)**
- **½ oz. fresh lime juice**
- **½ oz. Rich Demerara Syrup (see recipe on page 20)**

1. Combine all of the ingredients in a container and chill in the refrigerator.
2. Once the mixture is chilled, pour it into a SodaStream or Drinkmate and carbonate.
3. Pour the cocktail into a highball glass filled with ice and garnish with pineapple leaves.

TOASTED COCONUT AND OOLONG TEA CAMPARI: Combine 1 (1 liter) bottle of Campari, 30 grams toasted coconut, and 30 grams milk oolong tea in a container and allow the mixture to infuse for 6 hours. Strain and rebottle.

CHRISTIAN FAVIER, SEAHORSE

Seahorse is a seafaring-themed cocktail bar owned by and next door to Chubby Fish in Elliotborough-Cannonborough, Charleston, and it's one of the hottest cocktail tables in town right now. The eye of the storm is beverage director Christian Favier. Has he ever raised his voice in frustration? We don't know, but nothing seems to faze his cool-as-a-cucumber facade.

Calm, welcoming hospitality is one of his hallmarks, but his mantra is "everything matters." Favier asks, "There is no technique, or garnish, or ice, or type of glass that is a throwaway, right?" And he answers: "If every single element of the drink-making experience matters, then every single step of service and part of hospitality is really important as well."

Favier first rose to bar manager at Michelin-starred Junoon and Aquavit in New York City, and those experiences informed his culinary approach to mixology. He could pick the brains of great chefs, have access to incredible ingredients, and lean in to scientific methods for the bar that on the food side might look like molecular gastronomy.

"I've tried to bridge the gap between what people expect a cocktail to feel like and look like, including those feelings of familiarity and comfort and nostalgia," he says, "and also having things that are very modern and new and culinarily driven."

His cocktails have been featured in *Esquire*, *VinePair*, and *Imbibe*, and Favier's first tenure in the Lowcountry was at The Gin Joint. From there, he worked at The Ordinary for close to four years, expanding the rum collection for which the restaurant is known, before joining the Chubby Fish team at Seahorse, building a bar program from the ground up and including a Suntory Toki highball machine as its centerpiece.

However, the bar's menu obscures the in-depth prep for which Favier is known, and that is part of its charm. "If you need to list the technique for it to sound like a cool drink, then it's not a cool drink," he says. And Seahorse has some seriously cool drinks. "Trust is central with the guests. The responsibility falls back on us to make sure that what we put in front of them is great. You can't ask someone to do something outside of their comfort zone and then not put a lot of effort into it."

Butter-Washed Tequila-Mezcal: In a nonreactive container, combine 20 oz. Olmeca Altos Plata and 4 oz. Ilegal Mezcal Joven. Add 2 tablespoons melted unsalted butter. Place the container in a hot-water bath, or sous vide at 125°F for 1 hour. Bring the infusion to room temperature, then store it in the freezer for 24 hours. Strain the mixture through a coffee filter, making sure to leave the frozen butter behind, and then rebottle.

Umeshu Cordial: Combine 400 grams Choya Umeshu, 150 grams cane sugar, 8 grams citric acid, 5 grams sea salt, and 3 grams malic acid in a blender and blend on low for 2 minutes. Store the cordial for up to 2 weeks.

CHIAPAS PALOMA

SEAHORSE
254 COMING STREET, CHARLESTON

Seahorse is a stunning new cocktail bar by the Chubby Fish team, and the space, designed by Elizabeth Ingram, is a sultry seafaring zone on the bottom floor of a Charleston single house. Despite the cool addition of a dumbwaiter that ferries snacks from an upstairs kitchen, the star of the show is a Suntory Toki highball machine. Bar manager Christian Favier designed a menu of long drinks to showcase its bubbly potential, including this Paloma variation with plum wine and a hint of salinity in the glass, not on the rim of it.

GLASSWARE: Highball glass
GARNISH: Grapefruit slice

- **2 oz. Butter-Washed Tequila-Mezcal (see recipe)**
- **1½ oz. Umeshu Cordial (see recipe)**
- **4 dashes Fee Brothers Grapefruit Bitters**
- **Soda water, to top**

1. Combine all of the ingredients, except for the soda water, in a highball glass filled with one long ice cube.
2. Top with soda water, stir, and slide a grapefruit slice on the inside of the glass as a garnish.

TROPICAL NEGRONI

BAR GEORGE
1956 MAYBANK HIGHWAY, UNIT E, CHARLESTON

Just as it is in the rest of the country, the Negroni is popular in Charleston, and most bars in town can craft a solid rendition of the Italian classic. Creator Joey Goetz once called his Bar George bar program "cheap tiki—generally tropical but without all the elaborate bells and whistles." He gives the beloved Negroni the tropical treatment, switching out gins for split-portion fruit rums, trading the Italian loafer vibes for a sandy pair of flip-flops.

GLASSWARE: **Rocks glass**
GARNISH: **Orange peel**

- **1 oz. pineapple rum**
- **¾ oz. Campari**
- **¾ oz. sweet vermouth**
- **½ oz. coconut rum**

1. Combine all of the ingredients in a mixing glass with ice and stir.
2. Strain the cocktail into a rocks glass with a big ice cube and garnish with an orange peel.

RAPSODY

DALILA'S
441 MEETING STREET, SUITE F, CHARLESTON

Cocktail collaborators Alexander Duffy and Michael Whiteley were looking for a balance between smoky and fruity when they decided to build on a classic Southern Whiskey Sour foundation. What results is a smoky, sweet, and tart summer sipper that, despite its punchy personality for warm summer days, delivers in the booze department too.

GLASSWARE: Rocks glass
GARNISH: Mint sprig

- 1½ oz. Old Grand-Dad Bourbon
- 1 oz. Fresh Raspberry Syrup (see recipe)
- ½ oz. Banhez Mezcal
- ½ oz. fresh lime juice
- ½ oz. fresh lemon juice
- ¼ oz. blanc vermouth

1. Combine all of the ingredients in a cocktail shaker filled with a scoop of pebble ice and shake for 10 to 20 seconds.
2. Strain the cocktail into a rocks glass and fill with pebble ice, applying pressure to the ice to compress it and create a snow-cone effect.
3. Garnish with a mint sprig.

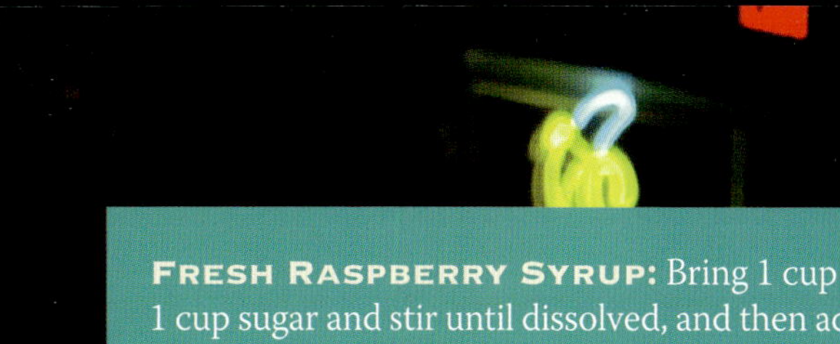

Fresh Raspberry Syrup: Bring 1 cup water to a boil, add 1 cup sugar and stir until dissolved, and then add an equal amount by weight of fresh raspberries. Allow the syrup to cool, then blend and strain it.

Moe's Bloody Mary Mix: In a large container, combine 1 (46 oz.) can of tomato juice, ½ cup Worcestershire sauce, ¼ cup hot sauce, 2 tablespoons horseradish, 1½ tablespoons Old Bay Seasoning, 1½ tablespoons celery salt, 1½ teaspoons fresh lemon juice, 1½ teaspoons fresh lime juice, and ½ teaspoon ground black pepper and stir. Store refrigerated in an airtight container for 7 to 10 days.

MOE'S BLOODY MARY

MOE'S CROSSTOWN TAVERN
714 RUTLEDGE AVENUE, CHARLESTON

Charleston is a Bloody Mary town—there are at least four companies commercially producing Bloody Mary mix here—but if you're drinking the cocktail out instead of at home, garnishes can quickly get out of hand, with everything from biscuits to baby crab claws perching on the edge of a pint glass. Moe's offers a classic counterpoint—fuss-free and downright delicious, just like their other bar-food classics, from burgers to buffalo tenders, served with a side of football games in season.

GLASSWARE: **Pint glass**

GARNISH: **Lemon wheel, lime wheel, olive**

- **Citrus juice, for the rim**
- **Tajín, for the rim**
- **1½ oz. vodka**
- **Moe's Bloody Mary Mix (see recipe), to top**

1. Wet the rim of a pint glass with citrus juice, then dip the glass in Tajín to give it a rim.
2. Combine the remaining ingredients in the rimmed glass and fill with ice.
3. Stir slightly and garnish with a lemon wheel, a lime wheel, and an olive.

MOUNT SAGE

THE ORDINARY
544 KING STREET, CHARLESTON

Inspired by the modern classic Chartreuse Swizzle, this cocktail swaps in a génépy for the increasingly rare Green Chartreuse, then adds a rum from The Ordinary's impressive collection. Génépy is made from the flowers of the artemisia plant, emulating the flavor of Green Chartreuse in a way most liqueurs can't (and it translates to "mountain sage," thus the name). Herbal, bright, and juicy, and with a cardamom kick, it's a Swizzle for a new age.

GLASSWARE: Collins glass
GARNISH: 2 bay leaves, bamboo straw

- **1 oz. Dolin Génépy le Chamois Liqueur**
- **1 oz. pineapple juice**
- **¾ oz. El Dorado 3 Year Old Rum**
- **½ oz. fresh lime juice**
- **½ oz. Falernum Syrup (see recipe)**
- **¼ oz. Rhum Clément Agricole Blanc**

1. Combine all of the ingredients in a collins glass.
2. Add crushed ice until two-thirds full and swizzle with a swizzle stick or barspoon until fully incorporated.
3. Add more crushed ice, creating a small mound over the top of the glass.
4. Garnish with bay leaves and a bamboo straw.

Falernum Syrup: Toast 4 green cardamom pods, crushed, in a pot over high heat until fragrant. Add 1 cup water and 8 fresh bay leaves, simmer for 5 minutes, and then immediately remove the mixture from heat and strain with a fine-mesh strainer. Add 1 cup white sugar and stir until dissolved. Allow the syrup to cool and store it in the refrigerator for up to 2 weeks.

Rose Petal Syrup: In a saucepan over medium heat, combine 1 cup water and 2 cups sugar and stir until the sugar is dissolved. Simmer for 5 minutes. Remove the syrup from heat and transfer it to a lidded container. Add 2 cups dried rose petals. Steep overnight, strain, and bottle.

ROSA MEXICANA

CATRINA'S TACOS & TEQUILA
834 FOUNDATION STREET #101, CHARLESTON

Gibran Trujillo-Pelcastre was taken by the bright pink known as Rosa Mexicano, a distinctive color name (first coined by author, fashion designer, and painter Ramón Valdiosera in the 1940s) that has now become one of the symbols of Mexican culture. Rosa also means "rose" in Spanish, so the mixologist combined the two ideas for this modern Margarita spin he serves at Catrina's off Clements Ferry Road. Although there are commercial rose syrups available, he stresses that the depth of flavor and natural color from making your own is essential.

GLASSWARE: **Rocks glass**

GARNISH: **Rose petals, dehydrated lime wheel**

- **Salt, for the rim**
- **2 oz. blanco tequila**
- **1 oz. fresh lime juice**
- **1 oz. Rose Petal Syrup (see recipe)**
- **½ oz. Cointreau**

1. Wet the rim of a rocks glass, then dip the glass in salt to give it a rim.
2. Combine the remaining ingredients in a cocktail shaker filled with ice and shake.
3. Double strain the cocktail into the rimmed glass, fill with ice, and garnish with rose petals and a dehydrated lime wheel.

GOOD OLD FASHIONED DP

PADDOCK & WHISKY
1074 EAST MONTAGUE AVENUE, NORTH CHARLESTON

Dr Pepper soda has a one-of-a-kind flavor, and Paddock & Whisky's general manager, Jeffrey Avans, should know—he drinks one daily. He created this cocktail for the Park Circle location (which boasts an impressive whiskey list and private tastings in an old bank vault too) as a tribute to his soda of choice, knowing that the soda's famous twenty-three flavors would pair well with this high-proof rum. What results is a more elegant cousin to the classic rum-and-Coke Highball, fancy enough to be served at your next cocktail party.

GLASSWARE: **Rocks glass**
GARNISH: **Orange peel, expressed**

- **2 oz. Mount Gay Eclipse Navy Strength Rum**
- **¼ oz. Dr Pepper Reduction (see recipe)**
- **2 dashes Angostura bitters**
- **Dash Angostura cocoa bitters**

1. Combine all of the ingredients in a mixing glass with ice and stir.
2. Strain the cocktail into a rocks glass over a big ice cube.
3. Express an orange peel over the drink, then add the peel as a garnish.

DR PEPPER REDUCTION: In a saucepan over medium-high heat, bring 2 parts Dr Pepper soda and 1 part sugar to a boil and allow the mixture to reduce until half the liquid remains. Cool the syrup and store it in an airtight bottle.

WHATEVER YOU SAY, STOVE

JACKRABBIT FILLY
1083 EAST MONTAGUE AVENUE, NORTH CHARLESTON

Jackrabbit Filly has a new, big space on Montague Avenue, with beautiful design details and an extensive menu. This cocktail, created by Will Moscowitch, is named after a line in the airplane scene of the movie *Bridesmaids*. It's a fitting moniker, since the drink is refreshing and humorously sneaky, resembling a Vodka Soda one might order on an airport day. Instead, Moscowitch's cocktail is full of delicate flavors, including pear, coconut, and a sweet, slightly nutty finish from the pandan, a leafy herb from Southeast Asia.

GLASSWARE: **Highball glass**
GARNISH: **2 lemon slices**

- **1½ oz. vodka**
- **½ oz. 1883 Pandan Syrup**
- **¼ oz. Purkhart Pear Williams Eau-de-Vie**
- **¼ oz. yuzu juice**
- **2 oz. carbonated coconut water, to top**

1. Combine all of the ingredients, except for the coconut water, in a cocktail tin with ice and shake.
2. Strain the cocktail into a highball glass filled with 2 lemon slices and pellet ice.
3. Top with the carbonated coconut water.

AGED EGGNOG

COAST BREWING
1250 2ND STREET NORTH, NORTH CHARLESTON

Coast Brewing was instrumental in growing the beverage industry in South Carolina by lobbying for higher ABV allowances. Aiden Merritt, son of founders Jaime Tenny and Dave Merritt, has grown up in the business and has now found that his passion lies more with a cocktail shaker than hops and barley, and his Aged Eggnog is one of the sweetest treats of the holiday season in the Coast taproom. He buys hundreds of eggs (the deep yellow from pastured egg yolks helps give the nog a nice, rich color) for his annual batches, but you can make a punch bowl full with fewer than a dozen. This batch makes ten servings.

GLASSWARE: **Nick & Nora glasses**

GARNISH: **Vanilla bourbon**

- **17 oz. organic whole milk**
- **7 oz. heavy cream**
- **100 oz. organic sugar**
- **11 pasture-raised eggs**
- **8 oz. Old Grand-Dad 114**
- **4 oz. Jamaican rum**
- **4 oz. Lustau East India Solera**
- **4 oz. Pierre Ferrand Ambré Cognac**

1. Work in smaller batches to blend the milk, cream, and sugar until everything is smooth and dissolved.
2. In a separate bowl, beat the eggs until light and fluffy, then fold them into the milk mixture.

3. Add the remaining ingredients and stir to incorporate.
4. Store the cocktail batch in the refrigerator for at least 1 month (3 months is the sweet spot) before serving, and garnish with vanilla bourbon.

SPA DAY

THE BETTER POUR
CHARLESTON

Megan Deschaine has been in the hospitality industry for close to twenty years and volunteered as the vice president of the Charleston chapter of the United States Bartenders' Guild for a decade of that. Her company, The Better Pour, serves a lot of Charleston private events and hosts a lot of bachelorette groups for mixology parties too, where ninety-five percent of the time, this cocktail is Deschaine's opener. It works with multiple spirits, hydrates, and is refreshing, especially during a Lowcountry summer. The Better Pour's bachelorette bashes are equal parts cocktail class, happy hour, and stand-up, and she says, "It still surprises me how many times I've left a booking feeling like I've made a bunch of cool new friends." You'll make new friends too, if you serve this crowd-pleaser.

GLASSWARE: Rocks glass
GARNISH: Cucumber ribbon

- 2 thick cucumber slices
- 2 oz. green tea
- 1½ oz. vodka, gin, or tequila
- ½ oz. fresh lemon juice
- ½ oz. Honey Syrup (see recipe on page 20)
- 2 dashes Scrappy's Lavender Bitters
- Sparkling water, to top

1. Muddle the cucumber in a cocktail shaking tin.
2. Add the remaining ingredients, except for the sparkling water, with ice and shake well.
3. To a rocks glass, add about 2 oz. of sparkling water, then strain the cocktail into the glass and top with ice.
4. Garnish with a cucumber ribbon.

SORRENTO SUN

SORELLE
88 BROAD STREET, CHARLESTON

This cocktail is built on smokiness with a bitter edge, and that's thanks to mezcal and Luxardo Bitter Bianco (which has a hint of wormwood, absinthe's main flavor). However, this cocktail is anything but bitter—it gets some sunny sweetness from passion fruit and carrot—befitting an elegant restaurant bar whose wide windows look out onto historic Broad Street.

GLASSWARE: Rocks glass
GARNISH: Dehydrated orange slice

- **1½ oz. mezcal**
- **1 oz. fresh lime juice**
- **¾ oz. Passion Fruit & Carrot Syrup (see recipe)**
- **½ oz. Luxardo Bitter Bianco**

1. Combine all of the ingredients in a cocktail shaker filled with ice and shake.
2. Fine strain the cocktail into a rocks glass over a large ice cube and garnish with a dehydrated orange slice.

PASSION FRUIT & CARROT SYRUP: In a container, combine 10 oz. water, 10 oz. sugar, 7 oz. passion fruit puree, and 3 oz. carrot juice, stirring until the sugar is dissolved.

METADETECTOR

MARBLED & FIN
480 EAST BAY STREET, CHARLESTON

Created by beverage director Kevin King, this introspective cocktail is a visual stunner, with its completely clear appearance around a vibrant red center. "The outer layer consists of nontraditional, Negroni-inspired ingredients, representing the present of the cocktail and how it's evolved," King says, while the center recalls the Campari element. "As you drink the cocktail, the 'past and present' combine to be both forward-looking and introspective."

GLASSWARE: Rocks glass

- **1 oz. Dolin Blanc Vermouth**
- **½ oz. Dimmi**
- **½ oz. Luxardo Bitter Bianco**
- **½ oz. Delord Blanche Armagnac**
- **¼ oz. Stoli Blueberry Vodka**
- **¼ oz. Sipsmith Strawberry Smash Gin**
- **Strawberry Consommé (see recipe), as needed**

1. Drill a hole in a 2-inch-square ice cube and place the cube in a rocks glass.
2. Combine all of the ingredients, except for the Strawberry Consommé, in a mixing glass filled with ice and stir until chilled and diluted.

3. Ensuring that the center of the ice cube remains unfilled, carefully strain the cocktail into the rocks glass.
4. Gently fill the center of the ice with Strawberry Consommé.

STRAWBERRY CONSOMMÉ: Wash and take the tops off 1½ quarts fresh local strawberries. Combine the strawberries and 2 oz. granulated sugar in a double boiler, and wrap with plastic film. Simmer for a few hours or until the strawberries turn white/gray and the liquid has been released, and then remove the double boiler from heat. Place muslin or cheesecloth into a sieve and strain the consommé. Measure and add equal parts Campari by volume to create a 50:50 blend.

BLACK MAGIC WOMAN

JACK OF CUPS
34 CENTER STREET, FOLLY BEACH

In the heart of Folly Beach, Jack of Cups is a haven for vegans and vegetarians, with its eclectic menu inspired by Asian and Indian flavors; therefore, it only makes sense that they'd have one of the most inventive Espresso Martinis in town. This cocktail, created by Ian Condon, uses two coffee spirits to add a deep coffee flavor, and that, along with the sake and amaro, really casts a spell. Don't skip the expressed lemon peel—it's definitely part of the magic too.

GLASSWARE: Coupe glass
GARNISH: Lemon wheel

- **1½ oz. Tozai Snow Maiden Nigori Sake**
- **½ oz. Mutiny Island Vodka Puerto Rican Coffee**
- **½ oz. St. George NOLA Coffee Liqueur**
- **½ oz. J. Rieger & Co. Caffè Amaro**
- **¼ oz. Coco López Cream of Coconut**

1. Chill a coupe glass. Combine all of the ingredients, except for the lemon wheel, in a cocktail shaker with ice and shake.
2. Strain the cocktail into the chilled coupe.
3. Express a lemon twist over the glass and around the rim, and then garnish with a lemon wheel.

GATOR BITE

THE RYDER CUP BAR
THE OCEAN COURSE, 1002 OCEAN COURSE DRIVE, KIAWAH ISLAND

Although The Ocean Course is an exclusive golf course to play, all guests are welcome to enjoy the exceptional view and the salt breezes at The Ryder Cup Bar. The most popular order is a Bagger Burger (*The Legend of Bagger Vance* was filmed on Kiawah's courses) and Gator Bite. During high season, the bar serves an average of two hundred of these citrusy cocktails a week, says general manager Alexandra Littlefield, making it the true legend of this course.

GLASSWARE: Rocks glass

GARNISH: Jalapeño slice, lime wedge

- **2 oz. St. George Green Chile Vodka**
- **1 oz. fresh lime juice**
- **½ oz. Cointreau**
- **½ oz. fresh lemon juice**
- **½ oz. orange juice**
- **½ oz. Jalapeño Syrup (see recipe)**

1. Combine all of the ingredients in a cocktail shaker with ice and shake.
2. Strain the cocktail into a rocks glass filled with ice and garnish with a jalapeño slice and lime wedge.

JALAPEÑO SYRUP: Bring 1 cup water to a boil, add ½ cup sugar and ¼ cup sliced jalapeños, cut the heat, and steep for 2 hours. Strain the syrup and store it in a closed container in the refrigerator.

MELON BALL

POST HOUSE
101 PITT STREET, MOUNT PLEASANT

This drink is a throwback to the late 1970s and 1980s, when the kind of balance we demand in cocktails today was far less important than bright colors, short recipes, and prepackaged ingredients. Offering someone this honeydew-hued cocktail today could "call into question their trust in you," says Lane Becker, an established Charleston bartender who has reimagined the club classic at Post House in the Old Village. "But they'll want a second one, and you will be glad you spent a whole day tracking down and prepping all this stuff." It's truly refreshing, with none of the classic sticky sweetness of the original.

GLASSWARE: **Highball glass**

GARNISH: **Skewered lime wedge and Luxardo cherry**

- **1½ oz. Don Q Cristal**
- **1 oz. fresh pineapple juice**
- **⅗ oz. fresh lime juice**
- **½ oz. Midori**
- **⅜ oz. Valdespino Deliciosa Manzanilla**
- **¼ oz. Giffard Orgeat Syrup**
- **Barspoon Suze L'Originale**
- **Barspoon Orange Sherbet (see recipe)**
- **5 dashes Angostura orange bitters**

1. Combine all of the ingredients in a cocktail shaker with ice and shake.
2. Strain the cocktail into an ice-filled highball glass and garnish with a skewered lime wedge and Luxardo cherry.

Orange Sherbet: Juice oranges until you have 500 grams fresh orange juice, reserving the peels and setting the juice aside. In a quart jar, combine the orange peels with 100 grams granulated white sugar, 1.5 grams powdered malic acid, 1.5 grams powdered citric acid, and 0.3 grams salt and let the mixture sit overnight at room temperature. Add the juice to the jar and stir to incorporate. Strain the peels out.

GAMECHANGER

HOME TEAM BBQ
2209 MIDDLE STREET, SULLIVAN'S ISLAND

Although Home Team now has six locations throughout the state and an additional restaurant in Aspen, it is still Lowcountry, through and through. In fact, for many locals, a perfect beach day has to end with a Gamechanger at the Sullivan's Island location, which also offers a spot to wash off the sand before placing your order. A Charleston cousin to the classic Painkiller, this popular drink has been served more than two hundred thousand times across all of the Home Team restaurants. This recipe makes a blender full, serving four.

GLASSWARE: Pint glasses
GARNISH: Freshly grated nutmeg

- **3½ cups strained orange juice**
- **1 cup pineapple juice**
- **¾ cup gold rum**
- **6 tablespoons water**
- **¼ cup spiced rum**
- **¼ cup Coco López Cream of Coconut**

1. Combine all of the ingredients in a bowl and whisk to incorporate.
2. Pour the mixture into ice cube molds and freeze.
3. Add the ice cubes to a blender and blend to the desired consistency, pour the cocktail into pint glasses, and garnish with freshly grated nutmeg.

SPICE GIRL

SULLIVAN'S SEAFOOD & BAR
2019 MIDDLE STREET, UNIT A, SULLIVAN'S ISLAND

Visit Sullivan's on a warm weekend night, and the front patio will be packed with people sipping on this easy-breezy cocktail. Created by Sullivan's bar manager Jordan Moton, it goes well with fresh fried seafood, a Sullivan's specialty. When infusing tequila, taste it every day or so until the desired spiciness is reached, keeping in mind that the agave and orange juice will balance some of the bite once the drink is constructed.

GLASSWARE: **Rocks glass**
GARNISH: **Lime wheel**

- **1 oz. blood orange juice**
- **Tajín Salt (see recipe)**
- **2 oz. Jalapeño-Infused Tequila (see recipe)**
- **¾ oz. fresh lime juice**
- **½ oz. Agave Syrup (see recipe)**

1. Wet the rim of a rocks glass with blood orange juice, then dip the glass in the Tajín Salt to give it a rim.
2. Combine the remaining ingredients in a cocktail shaker with ice and shake.
3. Strain the cocktail into the rimmed glass filled with ice and garnish with a lime wheel.

TAJÍN SALT: Combine 1 part by weight Tajín with 4 parts by weight Diamond Crystal Kosher Salt.

JALAPEÑO-INFUSED TEQUILA: Combine 3 to 5 jalapeño slices with 1 (750 ml) bottle of blanco tequila—leave in the seeds for extra spice—and allow it to steep at room temperature until it tastes as spicy as desired; then strain and rebottle.

AGAVE SYRUP: Dilute 3 parts by volume light agave nectar with 1 part by volume cool water.

PUKALANI PUNCH

COASTAL PROVISIONS
200 GRAND PAVILION BOULEVARD, ISLE OF PALMS

Created by Jessica Backhus, lead bartender at Wild Dunes Resort, to incorporate the best parts of a Mai Tai, Painkiller, and Rum Punch in one festive glass, this cocktail is served at the resort's restaurant, Coastal Provisions, during the summer months. Named after the Hawaiian legend that says that when it's storming all over Hawaii, there is a little break in the clouds over the town of Pukalani, it also applies to Lowcountry beaches, where if someone complains about a summer rain shower, a local reply is to say, "Give it fifteen minutes."

GLASSWARE: Tiki glass

GARNISH: Orange wedge skewered with a rum-soaked cherry, pineapple leaves

- **3 oz. Tropical Juice Blend (see recipe)**
- **½ oz. Flor de Caña Gran Reserva 7**
- **½ oz. Planteray Stiggins' Fancy Pineapple Rum**
- **½ oz. Novo Fogo Silver Cachaça**
- **½ oz. Pierre Ferrand Dry Curaçao**
- **3 dashes Angostura bitters**
- **2 oz. Jarritos Mineragua sparkling mineral water, to top**
- **Drop rose water**

1. Combine all of the ingredients, except for the mineral water and rose water, in a cocktail shaker with ice and quickly shake.

2. Pour all of the ingredients—including the ice—into a tiki glass, then top with the sparkling water and rose water.
3. Garnish with an orange wedge skewered with a rum-soaked cherry, plus pineapple leaves.

TROPICAL JUICE BLEND: In a large container, combine 8 oz. pineapple juice, 8 oz. fresh lime juice, 4 oz. Toasted Coconut Cordial (see recipe), 4 oz. filtered water, and 3 oz. Jack Rudy Cocktail Co. Grenadine. Store the blend in the refrigerator for up to 1 week.

TOASTED COCONUT CORDIAL: In a medium saucepan, bring 6 oz. filtered water, ¾ cup sugar, 2 tablespoons toasted coconut flakes, and ¼ teaspoon sea salt to a gentle boil. Stir to dissolve the salt and sugar and to prevent sticking, and simmer for 15 minutes. Cool and steep the cordial in the refrigerator for 24 to 48 hours, then strain and store it in the refrigerator.

BENNE GOODMAN

THE AZALEA BAR & GARDEN
219 SOUTH CEDAR STREET, SUMMERVILLE

The benne seed itself has a deep-rooted history as a prominent ingredient with West African origins. The benne wafer is a paper-thin, crisp sesame-seed cookie with a delightful blend of sweet, salty, buttery, nutty, and toasty flavor, and it's a Charleston culinary emblem. Mixologist Nathaliah Morant re-creates those flavors in the glass with a creamy, sweet cocktail meant for the end of a meal.

GLASSWARE: Collins glass

- **Sesame Sugar (see recipe), for the rim**
- **1½ oz. Hilton Head Platinum Rum**
- **1 oz. Toasted Sesame Syrup (see recipe)**
- **½ oz. Grimball Farms Smoked Pecan Liqueur**
- **½ oz. butterscotch liqueur**

1. Wet the rim of a collins glass, then dip the glass in Sesame Sugar to give it a rim.
2. Combine the remaining ingredients in a cocktail shaker filled with ice and shake.
3. Strain the cocktail into the rimmed glass.

Sesame Sugar: Combine 1 tablespoon sesame seeds, 1 tablespoon poppy seeds, 1 tablespoon light brown sugar, and 1 tablespoon sea salt flakes in a zip-top bag and shake.

Toasted Sesame Syrup: In a pot over medium heat, melt 1 stick salted butter. Add 2 cups brown sugar and 2 tablespoons toasted sesame oil and stir continuously to avoid caramelization. Stir until well blended and thick. Add 1 cup water and stir until the sugar mixture dissolves and no lumps remain. Store refrigerated for up to 5 days, rewhisking before use.

HABERSHAM PEACH

CRIOLLO
9 MARKET, BEAUFORT

Named after a prominent antebellum family who had ties both to this area and over the state line in Savannah, this cocktail screams "Deep South," despite appearing on the menu at Criollo, a tapas restaurant. (It is Beaufort, after all.) A variation of a Bourbon Smash, this drink celebrates a Southern summer delicacy—the peach. The caramel and vanilla notes of bourbon are a natural match made in heaven, or at least on a gracious wraparound porch where it's easy to catch a good sea breeze in the early evening.

GLASSWARE: **Rocks glass**

GARNISH: **Skewered peach slices, mint sprig**

- **1 ripe peach, sliced into chunks, skin on**
- **2 to 3 sprigs fresh mint**
- **2 oz. Elijah Craig Bourbon**
- **1 oz. peach schnapps**
- **1 to 2 oz. lemonade, to top**

1. In a cocktail shaker, combine the peach chunks and mint sprigs and muddle.
2. Add the bourbon and peach schnapps, fill with ice, and shake vigorously for 15 seconds.
3. Strain the mixture into a rocks glass filled with ice, top with the lemonade, and garnish with skewered peach slices and a mint sprig.

CATHEAD COOLER

OLD BULL TAVERN
205 WEST STREET, BEAUFORT

Old Bull Tavern is a true tavern, where locals and tourists meet to eat and drink, and the best action takes place at the long bar that stretches all along one wall of the main dining room. Partner Oscar Salas created this cocktail for that bar years ago, and it embodies the easy hospitality of the place, as well as capturing some classic flavors of a Southern summer: mint, cucumber, and honeysuckle. The key to it all is the distinctive Cathead Honeysuckle Vodka from Mississippi, a spirit loved throughout the South.

GLASSWARE: **Rocks glass**
GARNISH: **Mint sprig**

- **1 cucumber slice**
- **2 to 3 mint leaves**
- **1½ oz. Cathead Honeysuckle Vodka**
- **¾ oz. St-Germain Elderflower Liqueur**
- **Splash lemon juice**
- **Ginger beer, to top**

1. Muddle the cucumber and mint in the bottom of a cocktail tin.
2. Add ice and the vodka, liqueur, and lemon juice and shake vigorously.
3. Pour all of the shaker contents into a rocks glass, top with ginger beer, and garnish with a mint sprig.

LD BULL TAVERN
OBT
Beaufort, SC

SUMMER'S END

FARM
1301 MAY RIVER ROAD, BLUFFTON

The name of this restaurant says it all; each night, the menu features locally sourced food from the Lowcountry bounty surrounding Bluffton, and bar manager Cheyanne Ward gleans a lot of cocktail inspiration from the local farms too. She especially loves shishito peppers, and here, she pairs them with summer cantaloupe to balance out the bite, then adds a bit of smoky contrast with the urfa chile salt. It's light and refreshing, and with the cordial, it's easy to multiply the ingredients for a pitcher with friends on the porch.

GLASSWARE: **Nick & Nora glass**

- **¾ oz. fresh lime juice**
- **Urfa Chile Salt (see recipe), for the rim**
- **1½ oz. Bulrush Gin**
- **1½ oz. Shishito Cantaloupe Cordial (see recipe)**

1. Wet the side of a Nick & Nora glass with lime juice, then dip the glass in the Urfa Chile Salt.
2. Combine the remaining ingredients in a cocktail shaker filled with ice and shake.
3. Double strain the cocktail into the rimmed glass.

Urfa Chile Salt: Mix kosher salt with urfa chile flakes in a 3:1 ratio.

Shishito Cantaloupe Cordial: Weigh both 1 medium cantaloupe, peeled and deseeded, and 20 shishito peppers, sliced and stems removed; cut the melon into cubes; and place everything in a nonreactive container. Add an equal weight of sugar to the container, then add 2 teaspoons citric acid. Allow the mixture to sit in the refrigerator for 5 days, stirring daily. Remove the mixture from the refrigerator, add 1 cup hot water, stir, strain, and bottle.

BLOOD ORANGE GIN RICKEY

FISHCAMP ON BROAD CREEK
11 SIMMONS ROAD, HILTON HEAD ISLAND

Most guests arrive at Fishcamp, on Hilton Head, for the view, or the Lowcountry boil with shrimp and corn, but it's also a great place to toast to the sunset—the outdoor bar has one of the most storybook vistas on the island. The move here is this Rickey, made with gin distilled on Hilton Head and topped with CBD sparkling water called C Bubbles, made by Revival Beverage Co. in Charleston.

GLASSWARE: **Rocks glass**
GARNISH: **Lime wheel, rosemary sprig**

- **2 oz. Bulrush Blood Orange Gin**
- **Juice of half a lime**
- **CBD-infused sparkling water, to top**

1. Add the gin and lime juice to a rocks glass filled with crushed ice.
2. Top with sparkling water and garnish with a lime wheel and rosemary sprig.

ON'S
HEAD ISLAND

LOWCOUNTRY OYSTER SHOOTER

HUDSON'S SEAFOOD HOUSE ON THE DOCKS
1 HUDSON ROAD, HILTON HEAD ISLAND

A rite of passage in the Lowcountry, the Oyster Shooter is basically the melding of a Bloody Mary with the flavors of oysters on the half shell, and there are few places more picturesque to shoot one than Hudson's, located on a bluff with sea breezes, salt air, and sailboats streaming by. It also helps that the oysters served here are from owner Andrew Carmines's own Shell Ring Oyster Co. Salty, briny, and with a kick, these are easy to make.

GLASSWARE: **Shooter glass**

- **Old Bay Seasoning, for the rim**
- **1 oz. Deep Eddy Original Vodka**
- **½ oz. Zing Zang Bloody Mary Mix**
- **2 dashes Tabasco Original Red Sauce**
- **Dash cocktail sauce**
- **½ barspoon horseradish**
- **Freshly shucked oyster**

1. Wet the rim of a shooter glass, then dip the glass in Old Bay to give it a rim.
2. Combine the remaining ingredients, except for the oyster, in a cocktail shaker filled with ice and shake.
3. Strain the cocktail into the rimmed glass and add the freshly shucked oyster.

HARVEST MOON

THE INDEPENDENT
615 FRONT STREET, FLOOR 1, GEORGETOWN

Georgetown's historic waterfront district is charmingly walkable, and The George, a new boutique hotel in the district, is the place to stay to enjoy it. Elegant and a little eclectic, it has a rarity: direct marina access for those arriving by boat. This cocktail from The Independent restaurant within the hotel is reminiscent of a lovely autumn moon's color rising above that marina, with the salt marsh beyond. The drink's sweetness with a little spice is as intriguing as the view.

GLASSWARE: **Highball glass**
GARNISH: **Mint sprig, dehydrated lime wheel**

- **1½ oz. Novo Fogo Barrel-Aged Cachaça**
- **¾ oz. passion fruit puree**
- **¾ oz. Simple Syrup (see recipe on page 20)**
- **½ oz. Ancho Reyes Original Ancho Chile Liqueur**
- **½ oz. Cointreau**

1. Combine all of the ingredients in a cocktail shaker with ice and shake.
2. Strain the cocktail into a highball glass packed with crushed ice.
3. Garnish with a sprig of mint and a dehydrated lime wheel.

VISIT US
IN
SCHIEDAM
HOLLAND
Ketel One
BOTANICAL
Real Botanicals. Fresh taste.
PEACH &
ORANGE BLOSSOM
NO SUGAR
Ketel One
VODKA

PEACHY KEEN MULE

BETWEEN THE ANTLERS
100 WOOD STREET, GEORGETOWN

The deck is the place to be at downtown Georgetown's Between the Antlers, located on the Sampit River, with a view that can make having a cocktail almost a requirement. The simple answer is a perfumed yet easy-drinking Mule, easy just like the local scene here any night of the week. When fresh peaches are in season, consider swapping out the orange-slice garnish for peach, for a fitting topper to a summer day.

GLASSWARE: Mule mug
GARNISH: Orange slice

- **1½ oz. Ketel One Botanical Peach & Orange Blossom**
- **1 oz. orange juice**
- **Ginger beer, to top**

1. Combine the vodka and orange juice in a copper mule mug filled with ice.
2. Top with ginger beer and garnish with an orange slice.

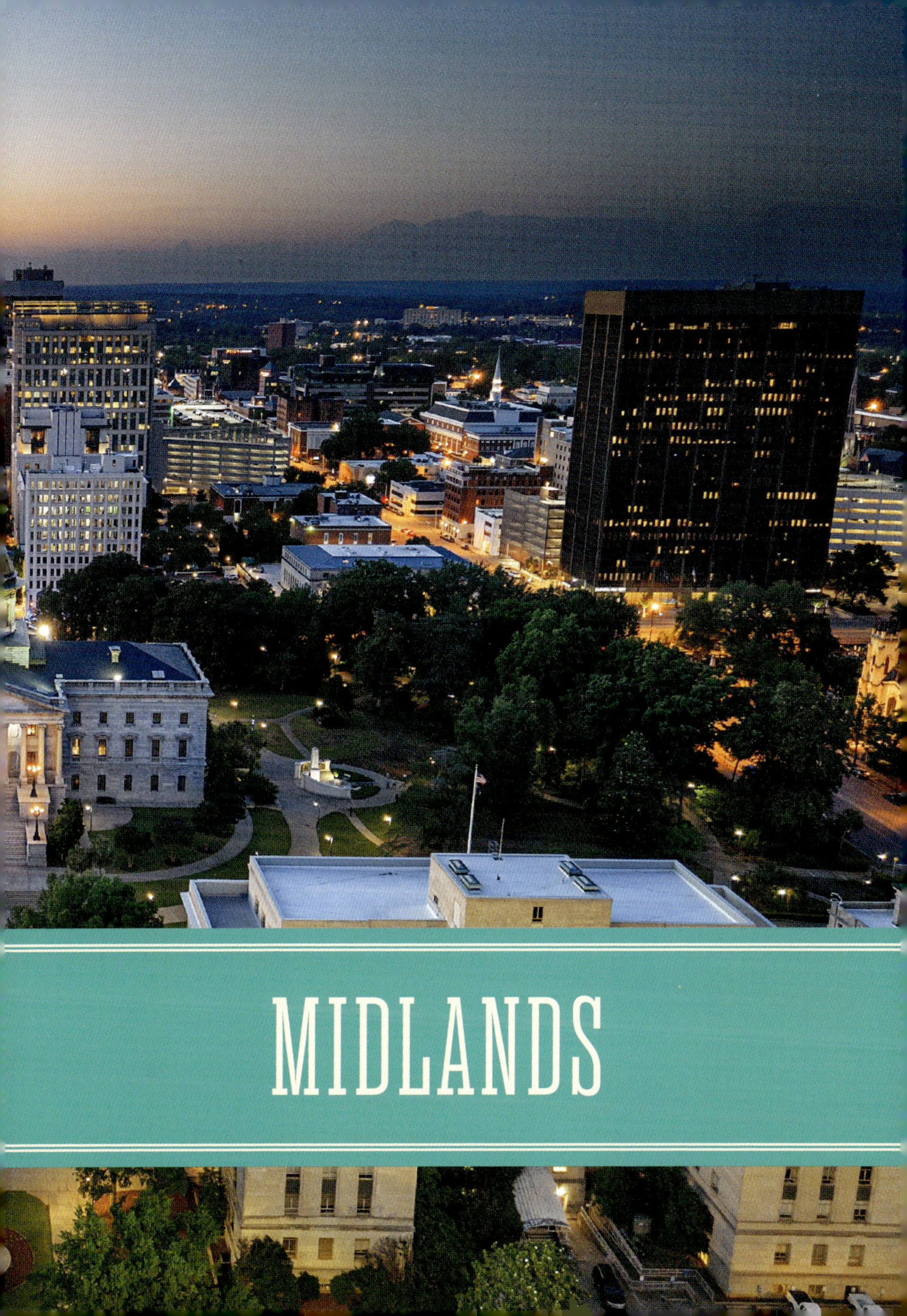

MIDLANDS

Island Boi

Heart of Darkness

Left on Read

Dirty Margtini

Dragon Mother

Camping at Dusk

Cinnamon Girl

Doctor's Orders

Cherry Limeade

Flor Picante

Pisco Sour

A Day at the Races

Rumpkin Stillskin

Pear Martini

Diablo at the Door

Embujado

In North Carolina, the area of rolling hills in the center of the state is called the Piedmont, but cross the state line to the south, and the name changes to the Midlands, along with the pace and point of view, even if the landscape looks deceptively similar.

Primarily made up of small towns strung along the I-77 and I-26 corridors, towns of note include Rock Hill, which feels increasingly more like a bedroom community for the behemoth Charlotte to its north, and Aiken, an equestrian enclave defined by two forces: horse racing and the Savannah River Nuclear Plant.

However, say "Midlands," and these towns are mostly afterthoughts—Columbia, the state capital, dominates the cultural conversation. For generations of South Carolinians, it's Five Points that is really the center of Columbia. The area is one of the most walkable in the city, full of independent businesses, public art, and, when night falls (especially on football weekends), a "party central" atmosphere because of its proximity to the University of South Carolina campus.

How does that translate to cocktail culture? Well, that means it's primarily a bourbon-and-vodka town, but restaurateurs such as Kristian Niemi and Will Green are pushing things forward while still managing to keep the crowds comfortable with their expanding choices, and creativity is on the upswing.

WILL GREEN, THE WHIG, WECO BOTTLE AND BIERGARTEN, THE HOOT

Will Green loves puzzles. As a bartender-turned-co-owner of three of the Midlands' most notable bars, he loves the idea of puzzles on puzzles when building a cocktail program.

"Each individual drink is like a little puzzle, and then the overall menu is like a puzzle," he explains. "For instance, when you're building out a menu you've got to make it work with all these different factors, from service style to how long it takes to make a drink, and combine that with the skill of the bartenders."

But it wasn't always like that. He once just really liked tacos.

"I came on at The Whig as 'the taco guy' for about a year; then I did one barback shift, and I was a bartender from then on," he says. Now closed, The Whig was one of the South's best-known dive bars, located steps from the South Carolina capitol complex in an old hotel building basement filled with taxidermy, bar food better than it had to be, and plenty of dark corners and strong cocktails. He eventually became a co-owner of the bar and, in the process, formed a partnership that led to the opening of WECO, West Columbia's open-air beer haven and bottle shop.

WECO is beer focused, so his generally "quiet" partner status gave him enough creative bandwidth to open The Hoot in Columbia's Rosewood neighborhood. Named after the owls that can often be heard in the area, it's another bar with a funky basement setting, bar food better than it has to be (vegan this round), and yes, tacos.

Green's approach to cocktail crafting is customer first. "Here in Columbia, it's bourbon and vodka. You know people are going to come in wanting those spirits, so then from a business and service standpoint, I want to have a vodka cocktail on the list. It's popular and a neutral base. Okay, then, the next question is how do I make it interesting for myself, creatively?"

Like many mixologists, that answer is building bar programs that have flavor complexity built into the prep work, not the actual building time during service. Green's menus routinely feature fresh herbs, shrubs, and clarified cocktails. His history at The Whig ingrained a high-volume approach, and it's still important to him to get a cocktail in front of guests as fast and efficiently as possible.

Green isn't a fan of what he calls "bartenders being the stars," but instead focuses staff service training on one mantra: customers are interesting. "You should be interested in your customers, and if you can do that, service takes care of itself. If you're genuinely looking around the room wondering about the people that you're surrounded by, then everything falls into line after that."

And when in doubt, be able to serve them tacos.

ISLAND BOI

THE HOOT
2910 ROSEWOOD DRIVE, SUITE 1, COLUMBIA

The Hoot, located in the Rosewood neighborhood, is known for its eclectic energy and vegan comfort fare. Although nothing can compare to co-owner Will Green's former haunt—The Whig—elements of its sisterhood shine through. It's a dimly lit kind of place where you can stay all night, with bright concoctions such as this one, which uses fresh strawberry puree for a true fruit-punch flavor.

GLASSWARE: **Rocks glass**
GARNISH: **Lime wedge**

- **1½ oz. Cimarron Blanco Tequila**
- **½ oz. Gran Gala Triple Orange Liqueur**
- **1 oz. Strawberry Puree (see recipe)**
- **½ oz. orange juice**
- **½ oz. mango juice**

1. Combine all of the ingredients plus ice in a cocktail shaker and shake hard.
2. Strain the cocktail over fresh ice into a rocks glass.
3. Garnish with a lime wedge.

STRAWBERRY PUREE: Place 1 pound strawberries, hulled, 1 tablespoon sugar, and 1 tablespoon fresh lemon juice in a blender and blend until smooth. Press the puree through a fine-mesh strainer to refine. The puree will keep for 1 week in the refrigerator, or freeze until ready to use.

Thai Tea Syrup: Steep ½ cup Thai tea leaves in 2 cups hot water for 5 minutes, then strain. Add 1½ cups white sugar and ½ cup light brown sugar to the tea and stir until fully incorporated.

HEART OF DARKNESS

BOURBON
1214 MAIN STREET, COLUMBIA

Originally created by bar manager Kat Hunter for the 2017 Woodford Reserve Manhattan challenge (winning second place for the Southeast division), this drink has been a top seller at Bourbon ever since. It has layers of deep flavor, changing as it warms. "While the title is obviously from the Conrad novel," Hunter says, "it came from me imagining a pensive hipster sitting at the bar, pondering life over this smoky concoction."

GLASSWARE: Brandy snifter
GARNISH: Hickory woodsmoke

- **2 oz. Woodford Reserve Double Oaked**
- **1 oz. Hoodoo Chicory Liqueur**
- **¼ oz. Thai Tea Syrup (see recipe)**
- **3 dashes Bittermens Burlesque Bitters**
- **4 dashes Bittermens Hellfire Habanero Shrub Bitters**

1. Combine all of the ingredients in a mixing glass and add ice. Stir for 15 seconds.
2. Using a Breville Smoking Gun, smoke a snifter glass with hickory wood chips, then cover the glass.
3. Pour the cocktail into the hickory-smoked snifter and keep it covered for 1 minute before the first sip.

LEFT ON READ

LULA DRAKE WINE PARLOUR
1635 MAIN STREET, COLUMBIA

Jessica Williams, director of education at Lula Drake, created this cocktail combining her and her husband's favorite predinner drinks to have when dining out in a new city. His favorite is a classic Last Word, and "personally, I am always a sucker for champagne before dinner," she says, which makes sense since her bar has one of the best lists of bubbly in Columbia. Williams combined the two, noting that it is worth it to use the good champagne in this one: "A little grower champagne can go a long way."

GLASSWARE: **Wineglass**

GARNISH: **Lemon twist**

- **¾ oz. Beefeater Gin**
- **¾ oz. Green Chartreuse**
- **¾ oz. fresh lime juice**
- **¾ oz. Luxardo Maraschino Originale**
- **Champagne, to top**

1. Combine all of the ingredients in a cocktail shaker with ice and shake.
2. Double strain the cocktail into a wineglass filled with fresh ice, top with champagne, and garnish with a lemon twist.

Extra-Virgin-Olive-Oil-Washed Tequila: Combine ½ cup EVOO and 750 ml of blanco tequila (such as Cimarron Blanco) in a container, stirring or shaking emulsified, and then allow it to rest for a few hours. Put in a container with a lid and freeze overnight. The next day, skim off any solidified fat, then strain the remaining liquid through a coffee filter and rebottle.

DIRTY MARGTINI

TERRA
100 STATE STREET, WEST COLUMBIA

Terra, a restaurant that has long been a Columbia bastion for local, seasonal cooking, has a philosophy of using simple techniques to allow an ingredient's full potential to shine. This cocktail reflects that philosophy. Although the idea of a "Margtini" isn't original, bartender Jordan McCormick gives it a simple twist by integrating the savory elements of a Martini with the fresh acidity of a Margarita.

GLASSWARE: Nick & Nora glass
GARNISH: Skewered olive

- ¾ oz. fresh lime juice
- Salt, for the rim
- 2 oz. Extra-Virgin-Olive-Oil-Washed Tequila (see recipe)
- 1 oz. olive brine
- ¼ oz. Madhava Organic Amber Agave

1. Chill a Nick & Nora glass, then wet the rim of the glass with lime juice and dip the glass in salt to give it a rim.
2. Combine the remaining ingredients in a cocktail shaker with ice and shake.
3. Strain the cocktail into the chilled, rimmed glass and garnish with an olive on a toothpick.

DRAGON MOTHER

THE DRAGON ROOM
803 GERVAIS STREET, COLUMBIA

"Every self-respecting cocktail bar needs an Old Fashioned," says David Adedokun, this cocktail's creator. For The Dragon Room, inspired by Japanese izakayas, he decided on a Japanese whisky version. "My aim was to highlight the flavor profile of Suntory's famed Toki whisky, while also providing some of the flavors a traditional Old Fashioned drinker would enjoy. The fire at the end adds a distinct flavor, but is also a great attention grabber."

GLASSWARE: **Rocks glass**

GARNISH: **Aromatic Orange Tincture (see recipe)**

- **2 oz. Suntory Whisky Toki**
- **¼ oz. Toasted Mandarin and Cinnamon Syrup (see recipe)**
- **3 to 4 dashes Szechuan Peppercorn Aromatic Bitters (see recipe)**

1. Combine all of the ingredients in a rocks glass over a large ice cube or sphere and stir 10 to 15 times.
2. Garnish with 3 to 4 sprays of the tincture, then light the tincture carefully with a small flame.

TOASTED MANDARIN AND CINNAMON SYRUP: Strain mandarins until you have ½ cup juice, reserving the husks. In a pot over medium-high heat, bring 1½ cups water, 2 sticks cinnamon, and the mandarin husks to a boil, then reduce the heat to simmer for 10 to 12 minutes. Add ¾ cup sugar and stir until the sugar is fully dissolved.

Strain and set the liquid aside. In a clean pot over high heat, caramelize 1 cup sugar, stirring constantly with a wooden spoon, being careful not to let the sugar burn. Add mandarin juice ¼ oz. to ½ oz. at a time, stirring carefully with each pour to incorporate. Pour in the cinnamon syrup, stir, and cool. This will keep for up to 1 month in the refrigerator.

SZECHUAN PEPPERCORN AROMATIC BITTERS: Add 1 tablespoon whole Szechuan peppercorns to 4 oz. aromatic bitters, such as Angostura. Let the mixture steep for 24 hours and strain.

AROMATIC ORANGE TINCTURE: Add the peels of 1 orange to ½ cup 100-proof vodka, allow the tincture to infuse for 2 days, and then strain and add it to an atomizer for use.

Muscadine Puree: In a blender, combine ¼ to ⅓ cup water to 1 cup deseeded muscadine grapes and puree until smooth.

CAMPING AT DUSK

MOTOR SUPPLY COMPANY BISTRO
920 GERVAIS STREET, COLUMBIA

Motor Supply Company Bistro opened in 1989 in the Vista, and it has been an important component of craft cocktail culture—and good food—since. This cocktail, created by Cass Herman, not only celebrates the muscadine, an old Southern grape variety, but the drink's beautiful varied hues also recall the deepening sunset at dusk in nearby Congaree National Park, the largest intact expanse of old-growth bottomland hardwood forest remaining in the Southeastern United States. This drink captures that feeling of late summer/early fall in the Midlands in a glass.

GLASSWARE: **Wineglass**
GARNISH: **Dehydrated lemon wheel**

- **1 oz. Muscadine Puree (see recipe)**
- **¾ oz. Campari**
- **½ oz. fresh lemon juice**
- **¼ oz. Licor 43**
- **¼ oz. Chambord**
- **¼ oz. Demerara Syrup (see recipe on page 20)**
- **Lambrusco, to top**

1. Combine all of the ingredients, except for the Lambrusco, in a cocktail shaker with ice and shake.
2. Strain the cocktail into a wineglass, fill with ice, and top with Lambrusco.
3. Garnish with a dehydrated lemon wheel.

CINNAMON GIRL

TAZZA KITCHEN
4840 FOREST DRIVE #20, COLUMBIA

Tazza Kitchen is a popular Forest Acres spot for drinks and wood-fired pizza in trendy Trenholm Plaza, and its cocktails are seasonal and always inventive. Tazza's beverage director, Lauren Spain, created this cocktail in 2018, when her love of Becherovka—a traditional Czech herbal liqueur—was running wild. It's an herbal, sweet, and spicy Margarita riff with coconut that feels as eccentric as the Neil Young song it was named after, and one that will be unforgettable for your friends on a winter's night too.

GLASSWARE: Rocks glass
GARNISH: Mint sprig, expressed

- **Cinnamon-sugar mixture, for the rim**
- **1¼ oz. El Jimador Blanco Tequila**
- **1 oz. Becherovka**
- **¾ oz. Spicy Cinnamon Syrup (see recipe)**
- **¾ oz. fresh lime juice**
- **¼ oz. Coco López Cream of Coconut**

1. Wet the rim of a rocks glass, then dip the glass in a cinnamon-sugar mixture to give it a rim.
2. Combine the remaining ingredients in a cocktail tin with a small amount of ice and whip shake.
3. Pour the cocktail into the rimmed glass, top with pellet ice, express a mint sprig over the drink, and then add the mint as a garnish.

Spicy Cinnamon Syrup: In a saucepan over medium heat, combine 2 cups Sugar in the Raw, 2 cups water, 2 chiles de árbol, and 3 cinnamon sticks. Simmer for 5 minutes, stirring occasionally to dissolve the sugar, and then cool, strain, and store the syrup in an airtight container in the refrigerator.

Black-Pepper-and-Sage-Infused Honey: In a medium saucepan over medium-high heat, toast ¼ cup black peppercorns until they become fragrant. Add 2 cups water and 8 to 10 sage leaves and bring the water almost to a boil. Add 1 quart honey and stir thoroughly to incorporate. Strain, cool, and store the syrup in a closed container in the refrigerator.

DOCTOR'S ORDERS

SMOKED
1643 MAIN STREET, COLUMBIA

Smoked is an impressively large restaurant housed in two Reconstruction-era buildings with multiple dining and drinking areas, including a tucked-away bar they call the speakeasy. General manager Jake Cooper created this, one of its most popular cocktails, around Bittermens Burlesque Bitters, which he loves for its unique combination of herbal aroma and vanilla notes on the palate. Additionally, honey helps the cocktail retain body when topped with soda, and if you prefer an extra-zippy drink, crack some fresh black pepper on top.

GLASSWARE: **Rocks glass**

GARNISH: **Sage leaf; expressed; lemon wheel**

- **2 oz. SKYY Vodka**
- **1 oz. fresh lemon juice**
- **1 oz. Black-Pepper-and-Sage-Infused Honey (see recipe)**
- **2 drops Bittermens Burlesque Bitters**
- **2 oz. club soda, to top**

1. Combine all of the ingredients, except for the club soda, in a rocks glass.
2. Top with the soda.
3. Add ice last and stir.
4. Express a sage leaf over the drink, then add the leaf as a garnish and garnish with a lemon wheel.

ART BAR

Columbia is a fairly traditional city where families and suburban life dominate, but nevertheless, it has a small but thriving counterculture at the intersection of visual arts and music. For many, the beating heart of this scene is Art Bar on Park Street, which opened in 1992 in the Vista, just when the arts-and-entertainment neighborhood was beginning to take shape. Currently owned by Andy Rodgers and Clark Ellefson, Art Bar is defined by its organic eclecticism, which has helped the bar remain relevant in Columbia for more than thirty years.

This spot is a kaleidoscope of color and textural interest weaving through multiple rooms, from its front-room bar lit with string lights and the ever-shifting graffiti filling the walls of its bathrooms to its eight Tobor robot figures that stand silent guard.

"Art Bar purchased the Tobor robots locally," says Rodgers, but they were originally manufactured in Atlanta by Robots International in the 1960s. The robots have come to be an important motif for Art Bar, and in Ellefson's work as an artist and craftsman as well—just recently, he created a 1,200-pound robot-head sculpture named *Fritz* that was installed in 2024 on the north end of Saluda Avenue in the neighboring Five Points area.

The connection Art Bar has with the community extends to its ever-rotating lineup of events, from Wednesday-night karaoke that packs the house to comedy nights or trivia, as well as a constant stream of musical acts that take the stage. Rodgers also notes that Art Bar has served its share of celebrities through the years, including Danny DeVito, Jack Palance, Kevin Bacon, John Waters, Gregory Hines, and Tony Hawk.

At Art Bar, the chicken fingers and fries always come out of the kitchen hot, the burger is best when it's oozing with melted pimento cheese, and the drinks are served fast and affordably. As the music gets louder, the dance floor often gets crowded, many dancing with drinks in hand as black lit robots silently stand by. Just a few blocks away, the State House regally meets the night sky, but inside here, this is another view of Columbia that is joyously different.

CHERRY LIMEADE

ART BAR
1211 PARK STREET, COLUMBIA

Although Art Bar isn't a craft cocktail hot spot per se, it is a true original, and this cocktail by Josh "Rosey" Rosenfeld is one of its most popular original concoctions, so much so that Rosey has an homage to it tattooed on his hand. Sweet, fizzy, and modeled after Sonic Drive-In's soda drink of the same name, the key to this cocktail is the cherry-flavored vodka. At 60 proof, it has a lower ABV than many vodkas on the market but can still sneak up on you.

GLASSWARE: Rocks glass
GARNISH: Lime wedge, maraschino cherry

- **1½ oz. Three Olives Cherry Vodka**
- **¼ oz. fresh lime juice**
- **¼ oz. grenadine**
- **Sprite, to top**

1. Place ice in a rocks glass, then add the vodka, lime juice, and grenadine.
2. Top with Sprite and garnish with a lime wedge and cherry.

FLOR PICANTE

COA AGAVERIA Y COCINA
823A LADY STREET, COLUMBIA

In a city where syrupy prepared drink mixes are still often a fixture behind the bar, finding a well-made Margarita can prove challenging. At Coa, the challenge is that a Margarita is just the beginning. The bar staff has high respect for mezcal and tequila, and that shines through in the careful craft technique and its delicious results. It truly is the best place in town when it comes to agave-spirit cocktails, and this cocktail illustrates the bartenders' skills, deftly balancing smoky mezcal with traditional Mexican flavors of citrus, chiles, and hibiscus.

GLASSWARE: **Coupe glass**
GARNISH: **Dried chile de árbol**

- **2 oz. mezcal**
- **1 oz. fresh orange juice**
- **1 oz. Hibiscus Syrup (see recipe)**
- **¾ oz. fresh lime juice**
- **¾ oz. Chile de Árbol Syrup (see recipe)**
- **1 egg white**

1. Chill a coupe glass. Combine all of the ingredients in a shaker without ice.
2. Dry shake to aerate, add ice, and then wet-shake to chill.
3. Double strain the cocktail into the chilled coupe and garnish with a dried chile de árbol.

Hibiscus Syrup: In a saucepan over medium heat, combine 2 cups water, 1 cup sugar, and 2 cups dried hibiscus petals and simmer, stirring, until the sugar is dissolved. Strain and bottle the syrup and keep it in the refrigerator.

Chile de Árbol Syrup: Combine 2 cups water, 1 cup sugar, and 8 to 10 chiles de árbol in a pot over medium heat and simmer, stirring, until the sugar is dissolved. Strain and bottle the syrup and keep it in the refrigerator.

Chicha Morada: In a large pot over medium heat, combine 1 gallon water; 4 ears Peruvian purple corn; 1 apple, cut in chunks; the skin of 1 pineapple; 1 cup sugar; 10 cloves; 3 star anise pods; and 1 cinnamon stick and simmer for 2½ hours, until the corn has become soft to the touch. Strain and let the corn mixture cool overnight. Add ½ cup lime juice and store the chicha morada in a closed container in the refrigerator.

PISCO SOUR

RATIO

566 SPEARS CREEK CHURCH ROAD #104, ELGIN

The inspiration for this cocktail was based on a favorite Peruvian juice drink—Chicha Morada, instantly recognizable in the country for its deep purple color. Executive chef Javier Uriarte always enjoyed this drink as a child, because it reminded him of fall and Christmas with all the baking spices it incorporated, and so he folded it into the house Pisco Sour, another staple in Peru. Here in the Midlands, this cocktail not only reminds the chef of his roots, but is also a delicious introduction to Peruvian culture for many South Carolinians.

GLASSWARE: Coupe glass

GARNISH: 4 drops Angostura bitters

- **1½ oz. quebranta pisco**
- **1 oz. egg white**
- **¾ oz. Chicha Morada (see recipe)**
- **½ oz. fresh lime juice**
- **½ oz. Demerara Syrup (see recipe on page 20)**

1. Combine all of the ingredients in a cocktail shaker with ice and shake vigorously.
2. Double strain the cocktail into a coupe and garnish with 4 Angostura bitters drops.

A DAY AT THE RACES

THE WAR MOUTH
1209 FRANKLIN STREET, COLUMBIA

Rosemary is used as an ornamental plant in many spots in South Carolina, and around The War Mouth's Cottontown neighborhood, it's easy to spot a bush or three, including in the restaurant's outdoor area. Bar manager Trish Vieler takes this easy-access herb and uses it to dress up a simple citrus vodka cocktail, right in line with the neighborhood vibe of this spot—this is a quenching sip no matter the season.

GLASSWARE: Rocks glass

- **2 oz. grapefruit juice**
- **Black salt, for the rim**
- **2 oz. High Wire Distilling Co. Hometown Vodka**
- **¾ oz. Rosemary Syrup (see recipe)**

1. Wet the rim of a rocks glass with grapefruit juice, then dip the glass in black salt to give it a rim.
2. Combine the remaining ingredients in a cocktail tin filled with ice and shake.
3. Strain the cocktail into the rimmed glass with fresh ice.

ROSEMARY SYRUP: In a pot over medium-high heat, bring 1 cup water and 1 cup sugar to a low boil, stirring to dissolve the sugar. Lower the heat to a simmer, then remove the syrup from heat and add 3 sprigs of rosemary. Cool, strain the syrup into a sealable container, add a fresh sprig of rosemary, and refrigerate.

PUMPKIN TEA SYRUP: In a medium pot over high heat, bring 1¼ liters water to a boil. Cut the heat. Add one box (or 20 bags) of Sweet Harvest Pumpkin Black Tea by Celestial Seasonings and allow the tea to steep for 10 minutes. Strain, then add 500 ml sugar and stir until the sugar is completely dissolved. The syrup will last refrigerated in a covered container for up to 2 weeks.

RUMPKIN STILLSKIN

OLD TOWN KITCHEN & COCKTAILS
300 TECHNOLOGY CENTER WAY,
SUITE #203, ROCK HILL

Just as in much of the country, pumpkin-spice mania arrives in South Carolina each autumn, showing up in all kinds of beverages and treats, often with sugary, cloying results. Leave it to master mixologist and Old Town beverage director Bob Peters to change the game with a balanced pumpkin cocktail that celebrates the season elegantly but still with a sense of humor. Peters, a Charlotte native, has won numerous awards (including 2015 Global Bartender of the Year for The Ritz-Carlton Corporation), and it shows here in every silky sip.

GLASSWARE: **Coupe glass**
GARNISH: **Orange peel**

- **1½ oz. Queen Charlotte's Reserve Carolina Rum**
- **1 oz. Pumpkin Tea Syrup (see recipe)**
- **½ oz. sweet vermouth**
- **2 dashes Angostura bitters**

1. Combine all of the ingredients in a cocktail shaker with ice and shake.
2. Double strain the cocktail into a coupe and garnish with an orange peel.

PEAR MARTINI

KOUNTER
135 EAST MAIN STREET, SUITE 101, ROCK HILL

Although Kounter has a new speakeasy named Elsie's, the best seat in the house is still the counter at this Rock Hill establishment. That's because this building wasn't always a restaurant—it was Mc-Crory's Five & Dime, where, in 1961, young African American students from nearby Friendship Junior College staged a sit-in at the segregated lunch counter. That counter still exists, lovingly preserved by the restaurant's owners, and a seat there with this bright, juicy cocktail is the perfect place to toast to better days ahead.

GLASSWARE: Coupe glass
GARNISH: Dehydrated pear slice

- 2 oz. Grey Goose La Poire Flavored Vodka
- 2 oz. pear nectar
- ½ oz. St-Germain Elderflower Liqueur
- 2 dashes Angostura bitters
- Juice of half a lemon

1. Chill a coupe glass. Combine all of the ingredients in a cocktail shaker filled with ice and shake vigorously for 15 seconds.
2. Double strain the cocktail into the chilled coupe and garnish with a dehydrated pear slice.

DIABLO AT THE DOOR

WHISKEY ALLEY
227 THE ALLEY SOUTHWEST, AIKEN

Whiskey Alley is a dark, cozy spot in Aiken's downtown, the place where burgers and smoked Old Fashioneds to accompany them just make sense. But so does this slightly smoky cocktail, created by Daniel Rodriguez Argiles, bar manager and mixologist. He takes the classic Margarita and adds two elements of spice (chile and cinnamon), which changes the summery cocktail into something a little cozier, perfect for that time of year when the sun is bright but you still have to wear a jacket.

GLASSWARE: Rocks glass
GARNISH: Dehydrated lime wheel

- **¾ oz. fresh lime juice**
- **Smoked Lime Salt (see recipe), for the rim**
- **1 oz. blanco tequila**
- **¾ oz. mezcal**
- **¾ oz. Cinnamon Syrup (see recipe)**
- **¼ oz. Ancho Reyes Original Ancho Chile Liqueur**

1. Wet the rim of a rocks glass with lime juice, then dip the glass in Smoked Lime Salt to give it a rim.
2. Combine the remaining ingredients in a cocktail shaker filled with ice and shake.
3. Strain the cocktail into the rimmed glass over a big ice rock, and garnish with a dehydrated lime wheel.

Smoked Lime Salt: Place ¼ cup salt in a smoker (using any kind of wood chips) for 1 hour. Grate the zest of 1 lime into the salt and stir to combine. Microwave the mixture on high for 2 minutes, until it is crumbly. Pulse the mixture in a blender briefly, then store it in an airtight container.

Cinnamon Syrup: Crush cinnamon sticks and add them to water in a 1-to-10 ratio by weight. Bring the water to a boil and then cut the heat. Add an amount of white sugar equal in weight to the water and stir until the sugar is dissolved. Allow the syrup to cool to room temperature. Store with the cinnamon, and strain before use.

EMBUJADO

RHUMBA RUM & CIGAR LOUNGE
321 RICHLAND AVENUE WEST, AIKEN

Elier Alberto's inspiration for this cocktail—Spanish for "bewitched"—was the Daiquiri, nodding both to his beloved Cuba and to his current home in the American South where the blackberry grows wild along the edges of woods and railroad tracks. The bar has a walk-in humidor, but if that's not your thing, ordering this easy drinker on the patio on a summer evening is a great alternate beginning to a rhumba evening.

GLASSWARE: **Nick & Nora glass**

GARNISH: **Skewered dehydrated orange wheel and blackberry**

- **3 blackberries**
- **1½ oz. white rum**
- **½ oz. fresh lime juice**
- **½ oz. Simple Syrup (see recipe on page 20)**
- **¼ oz. Chambord**

1. In a cocktail tin, muddle the blackberries.
2. Add ice and the remaining ingredients and shake.
3. Strain the cocktail into a Nick & Nora filled with crushed ice and garnish with a dehydrated orange wheel and a blackberry on a skewer.

62

PEE DEE AND GRAND STRAND

Pig in the City

Doctor's Orders

Blenheim & Bourbon

Fireside Sangria

Pepino Fresco

Orange Crush

Seablue Manhattan

Lavender Martini

Campfire Old Fashioned

Harvey Wallbanger

The Payday

The Pee Dee and Grand Strand areas are adjacent to each other, and while not quite the same in geography or general culture, they have a favorite flavor profile in common: sweet. The cocktail menus are dominated by either boozy (and most decidedly bourbon) offerings or sweet, often fruit-forward Funtinis and slushies meant to be served with a straw and a water view.

That's understandable. For a South Carolinian, summer is inextricably entwined with both of these regions, even though Myrtle Beach and its surrounding communities do have a lot of annual snowbird visitors and retirees. The Pee Dee's summer soundtrack is cicadas at the edges of sandy fields of corn, soybeans, peanuts, and cotton, where "driving into town" is still a common phrase that usually means Florence or Conway. On the plate are fresh vegetables, with steaks for date nights and fancy dinners, and before—or straight after—dinner, there are bourbon Old Fashioneds or Highballs with ginger.

Myrtle Beach—a partying destination for generations—anchors the Grand Strand, where the sounds of 1960s beach music gave way to big beachfront clubs and high-rises in the 1980s and 1990s. The best bartenders here don't shy away from sweet, but reimagine and refine it with fresh ingredients and modern mixology methods.

JAZZ ON DARGAN

Dargan Street runs through the heart of Florence's charming downtown, which is full of small shops and plenty of mid-century buildings. As night descends, the sidewalks get quiet—that is, except in front of Jazz on Dargan. This bar, owned by Thomas Mitchell and Neil McPhatter, is a beating heart of the Pee Dee town.

"Florence accepted this place with open hands," says McPhatter, who grew up in the hospitality business as part of Sylvia's Restaurant in Harlem, New York City, before relocating to the South. Jazz on Dargan hosts live music three nights a week, and McPhatter is the man behind the bands, booking acts to play in the front-window space. He's also more often than not the man at the door, checking IDs and taking cover cash.

Once inside, patrons pack the long, narrow bar with tables beyond, eating fried okra, wings, and oysters Rockefeller and drinking beer, cocktails, and green-tea shots. There's interaction, there's chatting, there's dancing, and there's always a good time. "We pride ourselves on the fact that whoever you are, hometown heroes, visitors, all nationalities come through this place."

PIG IN THE CITY

VICTORS
126 WEST EVANS STREET, FLORENCE

Located inside the beautiful boutique Hotel Florence, Victors's elegant dining room is the place for celebrations and holidays. Its bar hosts a charming mix of travelers, sports fans trying to keep an eye on the game, and well-heeled folks looking for a nightcap post some fancy event. In all of these cases, an Old Fashioned fits the bill. Beverage director Alan Free, a Florence native, is the mastermind behind this classic riff, a smoky, bacony sip perfect in a region that is known for its smoky, vinegar-laced barbecue.

GLASSWARE: **Rocks glass**
GARNISH: **Candied Bacon, smoke**

- **2 oz. Tasso-Washed Bourbon (see recipe)**
- **1 oz. Dolin Rouge Vermouth**
- **2 to 3 dashes Angostura bitters**

1. Combine all of the ingredients in a mixing glass.
2. Add ice and stir until well chilled.
3. Strain the cocktail over ice into a rocks glass.

TASSO-WASHED BOURBON: In a large container, combine 1 (750 ml) bottle of WhistlePig PiggyBack 100 Proof Bourbon and 1½ cups warm bacon fat and let the infusion sit at room temperature for 48 hours. Place the infusion in the freezer for 2 hours. Remove it from the freezer, then remove the congealed fat layer from the bourbon and strain the whiskey back into the bottle.

Candied Bacon: Preheat the oven to 350°F. Lay 8 strips Benton's Hickory Smoked Country Bacon on a rimmed baking sheet and thoroughly cover both sides of the bacon strips with 1 cup brown sugar. Bake for 7 to 9 minutes. Remove the bacon from the baking sheet and let it cool before serving. It can be stored in an airtight container in the refrigerator for up to 1 week.

DOCTOR'S ORDERS

TOWN HALL
101 WEST EVANS STREET, FLORENCE

Town Hall is one of the most beautiful places to enjoy a cocktail (and dinner) in Florence, not only because of its long, gleaming wood bar, but also because of its thoughtful and adept staff members who make having "just one more" an easy sell. This cocktail is served up in a rocks glass to keep the "take your medicine" vibe going with a cocktail meant to be sipped before it warms. The peaty smokiness of aged scotch mellows with sweet and bright flavors, welcoming more patrons to the enjoyment of the spirit, just like the spirit of Town Hall.

GLASSWARE: **Rocks glass**
GARNISH: **Dehydrated orange wheel**

- **½ oz. Giffard Ginger of the Indies Liqueur**
- **½ oz. honey**
- **½ oz. fresh lemon juice**
- **½ oz. Monkey Shoulder**
- **½ oz. Laphroaig 10**
- **1 to 2 dashes Scrappy's Black Lemon Bitters**

1. Combine the ginger liqueur, honey, and lemon juice in a cocktail shaker and dry shake (without ice) for 15 to 30 seconds to aerate.
2. Combine the two scotches in a mixing glass with ice and stir for 30 seconds with a barspoon.

3. Add the shaken ingredients to the mixing glass and stir 2 to 3 times.
4. Double strain the cocktail into a rocks glass with a big ice cube.
5. Finish with the black lemon bitters and garnish with a dehydrated orange wheel.

BLENHEIM & BOURBON

ELLIOTT'S
551 WEST LUCAS STREET, FLORENCE

A craft cocktail hiding in the costume of a Highball, the Blenheim & Bourbon is also the essence of the Pee Dee region in a glass. Acres of Jimmy Red corn, once nearly extinct before High Wire Distilling Co. helped bring it back into commercial production, are grown in the Pee Dee. The bourbon made from it has a distinctive creamy mouthfeel and notes of graham cracker and sweet baking spice, and it creates a deeply flavored cocktail when mixed with the sinus-clearing ginger heat of South Carolina's spicy Blenheim Ginger Ale.

GLASSWARE: **Rocks glass**
GARNISH: **Lime wedge**

- **1½ oz. High Wire Distilling Co. Jimmy Red Straight Bourbon Whiskey**
- **Blenheim Ginger Ale Old #3 Hot—Red Cap, to top**

1. Add the bourbon to a rocks glass filled with ice.
2. Top with ginger ale and garnish with a lime wedge.

FIRESIDE SANGRIA

WHITAKER'S
1025 3RD AVENUE, CONWAY

Ask many a North Myrtle Beach bartender where they like to get a craft cocktail, and they're likely to send you to Whitaker's, away from the beach. Located in a downtown area that is now hopping with new life, this neighborhood bar and restaurant is eclectic, with a menu ranging from sushi to truffle fries, and manager TJ Brister's creative cocktailing is a big draw. His menu shifts and changes, but this Sangria—deep and dark, with just a hint of gingery bubbles—is worthy of a heavy rotation during the cooler months.

GLASSWARE: **Wineglass**

GARNISH: **Orange slices; rosemary sprig, torched**

- **1 orange slice**
- **3½ oz. red blend wine**
- **½ oz. Simple Syrup (see recipe on page 20)**
- **½ oz. fresh lemon juice**
- **½ oz. brandy**
- **½ oz. triple sec**
- **Ginger ale or ginger beer, to top**

1. Muddle an orange slice in a small shaker tin.
2. Fill the tin with ice and add the remaining ingredients, except for the ginger ale or ginger beer, and then stir for at least 30 seconds.
3. Pour the cocktail into a wineglass and top with more ice if necessary.
4. Fill 1 centimeter from the top with ginger ale or ginger beer.
5. Garnish with orange slices and a torched rosemary sprig.

PEPINO FRESCO

CHIVE BLOSSOM CAFE
85 NORTH CAUSEWAY ROAD, PAWLEYS ISLAND

Pawleys Island's slow pace and sea breezes have been wooing visitors for generations. So, too, has the Chive Blossom Cafe, part of island life since 2002, and Natasha Sprinkle's cool cucumber cocktails are a preferred way to beat the heat after some fun and sun, especially under the live oak trees and twinkling lights in the cafe's courtyard. Simple to make on repeat all summer long, this cocktail is an easy way to prolong summer vacation, no matter the weather.

GLASSWARE: **Rocks glass**

GARNISH: **Skewered cucumber ribbon and lime wheel**

- **3 cucumber slices**
- **2 oz. blanco tequila**
- **1 oz. fresh lime juice**
- **1 oz. Simple Syrup (see recipe on page 20)**
- **Cucumber ribbon**

1. Muddle the cucumber slices in a cocktail shaker tin, add ice and the remaining ingredients, and shake.
2. Line the inside of a rocks glass with a cucumber ribbon, then fill the glass with ice.
3. Strain the cocktail into the glass and garnish with a skewered cucumber ribbon and lime wheel.

ORANGE CRUSH

BIG CHILL ISLAND HOUSE
4736 HIGHWAY 17 SOUTH, NORTH MYRTLE BEACH

This crushable (get it?) cocktail is a North Myrtle Beach variation on a drink that is much more common in the Northern United States. Big Chill Island House's parent company is in Rehoboth Beach, Delaware, so it makes sense that their menu includes this, but since it's South Carolina, bar manager Casey May gives the Crush a Southern twang by using Deep Eddy Vodka out of Texas. The result is an even deeper orange flavor that is a perfect cocktail for grilling out, pool parties, or just beating the South Carolina summer heat.

GLASSWARE: **Pint glass**
GARNISH: **Orange slice**

- **1½ oz. Deep Eddy Orange Vodka**
- **½ oz. triple sec**
- **Juice from half an orange**
- **2 to 3 oz. lemon-lime soda, to top**

1. Fill a pint glass with ice and combine the vodka, triple sec, and orange juice.
2. Top with the soda, stir, and garnish with an orange slice.

SEABLUE MANHATTAN

SEABLUE RESTAURANT & WINE BAR
501 HIGHWAY 17 NORTH, NORTH MYRTLE BEACH

The Grand Strand loves a steak house, and gravitates toward a sweeter cocktail flavor profile too, so meld those two traditions, and you have this Old Fashioned filled with warm baking-spice flavors. That's thanks to the sweet vermouth—imparting notes of cinnamon, bitter orange, and a little clove—which recalls old English-style Christmas desserts when paired with the ruby port–finished bourbon.

GLASSWARE: **Rocks glass**
GARNISH: **Luxardo cherries on a skewer**

- **2 oz. Angel's Envy Bourbon Finished in Port Wine Barrels**
- **1 oz. Vya Sweet Vermouth**
- **3 dashes Bittermens Burlesque Bitters**

1. Combine all of the ingredients in a mixing glass filled with ice and stir.
2. Strain the cocktail into a rocks glass with a large ice cube and garnish with skewered Luxardo cherries.

LAVENDER MARTINI

BAR 19 TWELVE
1912 HIGHWAY 17 SOUTH, NORTH MYRTLE BEACH

Located right on the main drag, Bar 19 Twelve is housed in the former Together Forever Wedding Chapel, which served happy couples for more than twenty years. Wedding chapels are still somewhat in vogue in the Grand Strand area, but this one now operates as a craft cocktail bar with a Pappy Van Winkle collection and all kinds of tinctures and concoctions behind the bar. This cocktail is as popular here as the lace on a wedding dress once was, and just as pretty, and the only commitment is whether to order another one.

GLASSWARE: Martini glass
GARNISH: Dehydrated orange wheel

- **1½ oz. Empress 1908 Indigo Gin**
- **¾ oz. crème de violette**
- **¾ oz. fresh lemon juice**
- **½ oz. John D. Taylor's Velvet Falernum**
- **½ oz. egg white**

1. Combine all of the ingredients in a cocktail tin filled with ice and shake.
2. Double strain the cocktail into a martini glass and garnish with a dehydrated orange wheel.

CAMPFIRE OLD FASHIONED

JOE'S BAR & GRILL
810 CONWAY STREET, NORTH MYRTLE BEACH

There are a few things that sincerely make Joe's unique. First, it's next door to a place called Hamburger Joe's, and they're not affiliated (so don't get confused). Secondly, guests routinely pack the place to enjoy prime rib and filet mignon while surrounded by the owner's extensive taxidermy collection, from swans to plenty of four-footed mammals. And speaking of mammals, the bar has a back deck called the Raccoon Bar, where guests can watch the black-and-white bandits amble out of the marsh to a feeder platform full of bread. This is what to drink to enjoy the show.

GLASSWARE: Rocks glass

GARNISH: Luxardo cherry, dehydrated orange wheel

- **Orange peel**
- **¼ oz. Simple Syrup** **(see recipe on page 20)**
- **Barspoon Luxardo cherry juice**
- **6 dashes Angostura bitters**
- **1½ oz. High West Campfire Whiskey**

1. In the bottom of a rocks glass, muddle all of the ingredients, except for the whiskey, without ice.
2. Add ice and the whiskey, stir to incorporate, and garnish with a Luxardo cherry and a dehydrated orange wheel.

HARVEY WALLBANGER

JEM SOCIAL
7601 NORTH KINGS HIGHWAY, MYRTLE BEACH

JEM Social has a lighthearted, subversively creative cocktail program, updating and re-creating some of the greatest hits (and some might say horrors) of bygone cocktail hours, in order to welcome a new generation while not ostracizing those who might be nostalgic for them. This Harvey Wallbanger from the disco-era list takes the classic vodka, Galliano, and OJ combo and ups the vanilla notes, deepens and balances the citrus flavors, and makes everything frothy with a double shake. Dust off that Galliano—this is a perfect way to keep it moving on the dance floor.

GLASSWARE: **Highball glass**

GARNISH: **Pineapple leaf and skewered orange slice and Luxardo cherry**

- **1½ oz. fresh orange juice**
- **1½ oz. pineapple juice**
- **1 oz. vanilla vodka**
- **½ oz. Galliano**
- **¼ oz. Cointreau**

1. Combine all of the ingredients in a cocktail shaker with ice and shake until chilled.
2. Strain the cocktail back into the shaker tin, discarding the spent ice, and give the cocktail a hard dry shake to create a fluffy texture.
3. Strain the cocktail into a highball glass with fresh ice, and garnish with a pineapple leaf and skewered orange slice and Luxardo cherry.

DEREK GOODWIN, FAT HAROLD'S BEACH CLUB

In the shadow of the high-rises of the Grand Strand, history is hiding. Before there was Boardwalk at the Beach or Ripley's Believe It or Not!, there was Fat Harold's, a Technicolor building that was the epicenter of shag dance culture on Ocean Drive. In fact, it still is, and beyond its beach music blaring into the parking lot or DJ Hall of Fame plaques on the wall, there's a thriving community. And its bartender is Derek Goodwin.

That said, using the term "bartender" for Derek Goodwin at Fat Harold's just doesn't seem fitting. He's Ocean Drive family. He even lives in a home willed to him by a former regular.

Goodwin grew up in the Ocean Drive area of North Myrtle Beach, affectionately known as the OD, and his childhood memories include the free, off-season spaghetti dinners or chicken bog nights for locals that Fat Harold's would host. His uncle worked at the shag-famous bar, and he lived within walking distance, so when he started working there, Fat Harold's felt like home. And that feeling has lasted for the last twenty-two years, even after Harold Bessent, the longtime owner, died in 2015.

"Every day I come in here and I work for him," Goodwin says. "As long as his name's on the door, I'll be here. I mean, I'm like part of the building at this point."

No one, including Goodwin, would categorize Fat Harold's as a craft cocktail joint. More often than not, his shift consists of mixing up thirty to forty shooters at a time—think Sex on the Beach or Melon Ball or Blond Headed Slut—then pouring them into little plastic cups all lined up on a tray. However, look beyond the cups or coolers of Michelob ULTRA, and it's easy to discover that, in fact, he is a master craftsman in the art of hospitality. He knows most of his customers by name and has their drink waiting for them by the time they reach the bar. He can work the grill on a busy Saturday night, making hot dogs or fried bologna sandwiches, and still not miss an order for a Vodka & Soda.

"Fat Harold's is a magical place, man," he says. "You can see people walk in on crutches, and when they get around the corner and they hear that music, they're eighteen again, you know?"

THE PAYDAY

FAT HAROLD'S BEACH CLUB
212 MAIN STREET, NORTH MYRTLE BEACH

One of the markers for a successful cocktail shooter is that it tastes like a food, from a piece of candy to a peanut-butter-and-jelly sandwich. This Fat Harold's mainstay—especially popular during the annual Society of Stranders Spring Safari—was created to be reminiscent of a Payday candy bar, which is sweet nougat surrounded by salted peanuts. The bartenders at the shag dance mecca make hundreds of these a year to keep the dance floor hopping.

GLASSWARE: Shot glasses

- **Salt, for the rims**
- **2 oz. Frangelico**
- **2 oz. butterscotch schnapps**

1. Wet the rims of two shot glasses, then dip them in salt to give them a rim. Combine the remaining ingredients in a cocktail tin with ice and shake until chilled.
2. Strain the cocktail into the rimmed glasses.

BACKYARD DISTILLERY

For much of South Carolina's history, moonshine distilling was a vital source of income for those skilled enough to both create spirits and evade the law while doing it. Subsistence farming or sharecropping was just not enough to sustain a family, so earning additional income from making moonshine was a common way to amend the family's finances. This was especially true in the Pee Dee region, where father and son Harrison and Howard Conyers are keeping the tradition alive—legally—through Backyard Distillery in Manning.

Harrison worked for years growing and grinding corn, as well as repairing distilling and farming equipment, and his son, Howard, remembers his chore of grinding cornmeal as part of his youth. He didn't realize until much later that some of that cornmeal did, in fact, go to bootleggers for moonshine production.

The Conyerses' microdistillery opened in 2020 with hand-built stills on the farm that Harrison still works. "The farm thing is important," says Howard, who was an engineer in New Orleans before relocating home to South Carolina. "Getting back to my roots, in all of it, I'm getting back to who I am as a person."

They distill what they grow, from corn to heirloom sweet potatoes that are widely regarded as some of the best in the county, and some of the 'shine is even aged in a barrel. Most, though, is clear through and through and bottled in mini milk jugs that pay homage to the Black tradition of moonshine in plastic milk jugs. "There's an art to making alcohol in a pot still, and if you're using a simple pot still with direct heat, just like barbecue, you have to watch the fire," says Howard.

For now, the company's spirits are mainly available for sale at the farm and through special events, but as the Conyerses continue to hone their craft and develop new products, that could change.

UPSTATE

Sherry Baby

Farmhouse Fizz

Mountain Water

Bless Your Heart

Rich Girl

Hugo Spritz

Pirate Talk

Rosé Cheeks

Trappe Door Whiskey Sour

Mezcaluna

The Traveler

The Lady Diana

Summer Lovin

Sir Percy

Dew Beginning

The Golden Hour

Poor Little Rich Girl

Audrey II

Blueberry Limoncello Martini

Rhubarbra

Baja Blast

The Tiramisu Cocktail

El Chupacabra

The Blue Ridge Mountains in South Carolina have their share of high peaks and dark valleys full of rhododendrons, winding creeks, and waterfalls, but when it comes to cocktails, the Foothills are where they're found. While Spartanburg (sometimes referred to wryly as Sparkle City) has a few glimmers of creative cocktailing, Greenville-area bartenders are only getting better, fueled by their growing camaraderie and the discretionary spending of new residents—many with international roots—who have relocated or visit as part of the burgeoning tech and automotive industries here.

Case in point, Greenville's gin moment—which, of course, with its varied styles and botanicals, is a good sign that area bartenders have joined the larger cocktail culture conversation. Add to that some spotting of tiki-style, amaro-driven, or clarified concoctions, and it's easy to conclude that the Upstate is a great place to grab a drink.

Weaving together Greenville's craft beer culture with Upstaters' love of cycling and the outdoors is the Swamp Rabbit Trail, a twenty-eight-mile walking and cycling greenway that runs along the Reedy River and connects the city to the town of Travelers Rest. It's a good-weather pastime to go barhopping by bike on the trail. The trail is also accessible by Greenlink, Greenville's public transit, which accommodates bikes as well, making the system a shining jewel of the Upstate, connecting craft brews and cocktails, community, and communing with the outdoors into a worthy weekend pursuit.

THE RABBIT HOLE

Reclaimed wood doors, age-fogged mirrors, moss on the walls, and vining plants trailing from dark corners around twinkling lights and candelabras: This is the world of The Rabbit Hole, located in The Village of West Greenville, the city's arts district, where the cocktails are often served in teacups, there's a library speakeasy with a separate menu, and you can listen to Alice and Wonderland on a loop in the bathroom.

The brainchild of Greenville contractor Sebastian Carter—who, along with David Marshall of DM2 Furnishings, hand built much of the elements of the space—The Rabbit Hole is a reimagining of the world of Lewis Carroll's *Alice in Wonderland*, where "all the best people are a little mad." Carter is a native of Cheshire, England—the home of *Alice* author Lewis Carroll—and his bar decor, where Victoriana meets lush garden landscape, has evolved over time, with not only the owners and staff layering elements into the space, but also guests often getting in on the act.

"Our regulars will bring in *Alice in Wonderland* books or other mementos, saying, 'This made us think of you,' and it really adds to that personal feel that we're trying to create here," says bar manager Kate Kavanaugh.

The offerings have also slowly evolved since The Rabbit Hole opened in 2022, moving from more of a wine bar format into a formal cocktail-program focus, with a separate and more spirit-forward menu in the library. The shift has allowed staff members to spread their wings creatively and join the larger cocktail-crafting conversation that is gaining steam in Greenville. However, despite their commitment to craft, the childlike wonder of the book's aesthetic grounds them and keeps them from getting too precious about particular ingredients or presentation. For example, Kavanaugh always makes sure there's at least one cocktail on the menu served in a teacup, and she's always quick to accommodate additional teacup requests.

"It's such a fun little silly moment to bring someone an Old Fashioned in a teacup and watch their face light up." And down the rabbit hole they go.

SHERRY BABY

THE RABBIT HOLE
1268 PENDLETON STREET, GREENVILLE

The Rabbit Hole takes the *Alice in Wonderland* theme to heart, so it makes sense that there is always a cocktail served in a teacup on the menu (and if you prefer, any other cocktail you desire served in one too, upon request), but this sweet sip is especially fitting for your next Mad Hatter encounter. It features sloe gin, a liqueur created in rural seventeenth-century England, where sloe berries (a kind of plum) grow wild in the hedgerows.

GLASSWARE: **Teacup**

- **1½ oz. Hayman's Sloe Gin**
- **1 oz. New Amsterdam Stratusphere Original Gin**
- **¼ oz. John D. Taylor's Velvet Falernum**
- **¼ oz. Valdespino Tio Diego Amontillado**

1. Combine all of the ingredients in a mixing glass filled with ice and stir.
2. Strain the cocktail into a teacup.

JANETTE WESLEY, VICARIO MICRO-DISTILLERY AND FARM

It always begins in the garden for Janette Wesley of VICARIO Micro-Distillery and Farm. A native of Greenville, she's had her hands in the dirt for most of her life, and through years of sun and rain, frosts and planting days, she has developed into a professional gardener. Her habit of paying attention to what grows well in the microclimates of the garden behind the distillery in Greer, or on a slope that gets afternoon sun at Villa Sant'Andrea (her Italian home near Cortona), has developed into a rhythm of her life of planning, planting, and harvesting—and for the last twelve years, making spirits in Greer.

Sustainably grown and organic botanicals are at the heart of everything VICARIO makes, and as such, the company grows many of the botanicals itself, on two continents. The delicate perfume of olive leaves takes center stage in the Olive Leaf Liqueur, adapted from an ancient Roman recipe; more than fifteen herbs and spices—including estate-grown black peppermint, the warmth of myrrh, and French tarragon—are blended into the Monk's Secret Liqueur; and bright fruit flavors, from wild sour cherry to Seville orange, are made with whole, organic ingredients, resulting in liqueurs that are the essence of freshly pressed fruit instead of cloyingly sweet and syrupy. All in all, VICARIO produces twenty-one small-batch spirits, as well as limited batches of olive oil, at its Greer facility.

VICARIO was a joint venture between Wesley and her husband, Renato Vicario, until he passed away last year. She was the gardener, and he was the cook and recipe developer. "That's just kind of how we worked it all out," she says.

Vicario was a Sommelier Clos de Vougeot and Compagnon de Bordeaux and lived in many countries across the globe through his forty-five years as a world culture, gastronomic, and heritage travel wholesaler, and he was deeply passionate about history and culture. He wrote *Italian Liqueurs: History and Art of a Creation*, and he prized

VICARIO
Nocino Walnut Liqueur
PRODUCT OF USA
Coffee Liq
PRODUCT OF

historical recipes, rare fruits, and traditional liqueur-making techniques in his pursuit of flavor.

The handcrafted spirits that VICARIO produces have a cult following with bartenders in the know throughout the country (especially in California and New York) and have been featured in *Food & Wine*, *VinePair*, and *Punch*. The spirits are truly unique, showcasing the complexity and subtlety of natural ingredients in an American liqueur landscape that's flooded with products using synthetic coloring and flavorings.

"We did things together, so I learned a lot about how his whole thought process went when he was putting his recipe together," Wesley explains. "I learned a lot about tasting from him, so that has helped me now that he's not there. It was really daunting to try and step into his shoes as well as stay in my own, but I've managed to do it, and I feel he would be really proud of me."

While Vicario left some recipes that had not been produced, Wesley hasn't tried her hand at making them—yet. Instead, she is venturing into this new phase by beginning where she always does—in the garden.

Right now, she's working on growing a very specific Italian poppy variety in South Carolina for its dried petals and planning to process one of the last recipes that Renato Vicario left, his own fernet. Although extremely complex, she will attempt the challenge he left her, never straying from their principles of excellence. It's already taken one growing season to collect enough poppy petals, as well as the threads of saffron, and there's always something to do for the next season, the next bottling, the next recipe. She knows that the rhythm of the garden will assist her as it always has.

"Renato said constantly that all that's involved in this process takes time, you know, and you have to be patient." That patience is what liqueur making the VICARIO way is all about, and the results are evident in every sip.

Olive Oil–Washed Gin: In a wide container, combine 4 oz. VICARIO Olive Oil and 1 (750 ml) bottle of VICARIO Gin. Freeze the infusion overnight, scrape off the frozen fat content, strain the gin through a chinois and coffee filter, and rebottle.

FARMHOUSE FIZZ

ENTRE NOUS
104 SOUTH MAIN STREET, GREENVILLE

A speakeasy tucked behind Maestro Bistro & Dinner Club in downtown Greenville, Entre Nous is helmed by bar manager Adam Kirwan. "I was born and raised in Greer, so it's amazing to not only see a masterpiece production, but also to see the level of detail VICARIO goes to, to bring exceptionally fine liqueurs and spirits to the Upstate and beyond," Kirwan says. This cocktail features multiple spirits by the local company, as well as an oil-washed gin, providing a silky, creamy undertone while not necessarily changing the botanicals and profiles of the base spirit.

GLASSWARE: Wineglass
GARNISH: Mint sprig

- **5 mint leaves**
- **1½ oz. Olive Oil–Washed Gin (see recipe)**
- **¾ oz. fresh lime juice**
- **¾ oz. VICARIO Olive Leaf Liqueur**
- **1 oz. VICARIO Mirto Liqueur**
- **1 oz. Demerara Syrup (see recipe on page 20)**
- **Prosecco, to top**
- **Club soda, to top**

1. Smack the mint leaves to release the oils, then combine them and the remaining ingredients, except for the prosecco and club soda, in a cocktail shaker filled with ice and shake.
2. Strain the cocktail into a wineglass filled with ice, top with equal parts prosecco and club soda, and garnish with a mint sprig.

MOUNTAIN WATER

RESTAURANT 17
10 ROAD OF VINES, TRAVELERS REST

Located within the Hotel Domestique, a beautiful boutique hotel inspired by the world travels of cyclist George Hincapie, Restaurant 17 is a fine-dining destination that is used to catering to those who love the good life—and love living it out of doors as much as possible. Refreshing as if from a cold mountain stream, this cocktail is crisp and bright with a touch of herbaceous complexity, and it's the perfect end to a long cycling day.

GLASSWARE: Rocks glass
GARNISH: Rosemary sprig

- **1½ oz. High Wire Distilling Co. Hat Trick Gin**
- **¾ oz. Dolin Blanc Vermouth**
- **½ oz. Rosemary Syrup (see recipe)**
- **½ oz. fresh lemon juice**
- **2 tablespoons diluted honey**

1. Combine all of the ingredients in a cocktail shaker filled with ice and shake.
2. Double strain the cocktail into a rocks glass over a large ice cube and garnish with a rosemary sprig.

ROSEMARY SYRUP: Combine 1 quart sugar, 1 quart water, and 1 bunch of rosemary in a pot, bring the mixture to a boil, and then lower the heat and simmer for 5 to 10 minutes. Cool and strain the syrup, then store it in a covered container in the refrigerator for 7 to 10 days.

Apple-Infused Bourbon: Peel and core 2 fresh medium-size apples, then combine them with 1 (750 ml) bottle of bourbon. Steep for approximately 72 hours, strain, and rebottle.

BLESS YOUR HEART

INDACO GREENVILLE
40 WEST BROAD STREET, GREENVILLE

Greenville sits in the foothills of the Southern Appalachian Mountains, a region known for its affinity for apples and ability to grow them exceptionally well. The restaurant's mixologist, Deb Cabe, created this cocktail to celebrate the regional fruit, highlighting the sweet crispness of an in-season apple with its natural companion: brown sugar. This cocktail brings to life crisp fall days in the foothills, when it's time to light the first fire in the fireplace.

GLASSWARE: Coupe glass
GARNISH: Apple slice

- **Brown sugar, for the rim**
- **1½ oz. Apple-Infused Bourbon (see recipe)**
- **¼ oz. Frangelico**
- **¼ oz. Grand Marnier**
- **¼ oz. orgeat**
- **¼ oz. Honey Syrup (see recipe on page 20)**
- **¼ oz. fresh lemon juice**
- **¼ oz. Cardamaro**

1. Wet the rim of a coupe glass, then dip the glass in brown sugar to give it a rim.
2. Combine the remaining ingredients in a cocktail shaker with ice and shake thoroughly.
3. Double strain the cocktail into the rimmed glass and garnish with a thin apple slice.

RICH GIRL

JUNIPER
315 SOUTH MAIN STREET, GREENVILLE

Juniper's bestseller, named after the Hall & Oates song, is a sweet yet complex cocktail. The Cava Foam helps dry out the drink so that the rich syrup is not too overpowering—plus it's fun to make. Creator Baileigh Wilson chose a faux engagement ring as a garnish to be a bit cheeky and over-the-top, but it also adds complexity. The bar staff has noticed that on occasion, cocktail sippers mistakenly take it for a real proposal, complicating things for a significant other present.

GLASSWARE: Coupe glass
GARNISH: Plastic diamond ring

- **1½ oz. The Botanist Islay Dry Gin**
- **1 oz. Combier Crème de Framboise**
- **¾ oz. Rich Vanilla Bean Lavender Syrup (see recipe)**
- **¾ oz. fresh lemon juice**
- **Cava Foam (see recipe), to top**

1. Combine all of the ingredients, except for the foam, in a cocktail shaker with ice and shake.
2. Strain the cocktail into a coupe, top with Cava Foam, and garnish with a faux engagement ring.

Rich Vanilla Bean Lavender Syrup: In a saucepan over medium-high heat, combine 16 oz. Sugar in the Raw, 8 oz. water, 4 oz. vanilla bean paste, and a small handful of dried lavender flowers and bring the mixture to a boil. Lower the heat and simmer for 10 minutes, then cool, strain, and store the syrup in an airtight bottle.

Cava Foam: In a blender, combine 200 ml water, 40 grams agar, and 11 grams dried egg white powder and blend. Transfer the mixture to a larger container and slowly pour in 1 (750 ml) bottle of cava. Fill a foaming canister to the limit with the mixture and charge twice before using.

HUGO SPRITZ

JIANNA
600 SOUTH MAIN STREET #2, GREENVILLE

Andrea Royko, general manager/managing partner at Jianna, feels that Italian cocktails are still underrated in America. She says, "They can be so diverse, from bitter and digestive to sweet and bubbly." Royko showcases the latter here, in a springtime sip that is an effervescent way to begin a meal of seasonal Italian dishes from executive chef Michael Kramer, who recently released the Jianna cookbook.

GLASSWARE: **Wineglass**

GARNISH: **Lemon slice, mint leaves**

- **4 mint leaves**
- **¾ oz. elderflower liqueur**
- **2½ oz. dry prosecco**
- **Lemon wedge**

1. In a wineglass, muddle the mint leaves and liqueur.
2. Add ice, top with the prosecco, and stir gently.
3. Garnish with a lemon slice and mint leaves, then squeeze the lemon wedge into the drink and discard.

PIRATE TALK

WOODSIDE BISTRO
HISTORIC LOFTS AT WOODSIDE MILL, EAST 5TH STREET, GREENVILLE

When Woodside Bistro moved from their original location on Woodside Avenue to their current location within the historic mill complex, they upped the ante on the bar program with delicious results. Bar team Michael Grissinger and Roby Hubbard collaborate on menus and drinks, including this one in their favorite genre: tiki. While many banana-centric cocktails can be too much of a good thing, this combo of Irish whiskey infused with banana provides a solid foundation for a balanced, beachy sipper in the middle of the Carolina foothills.

GLASSWARE: Parfait glass

GARNISH: Orange slice, freshly grated nutmeg

- **1½ oz. Banana-Infused Irish Whiskey (see recipe)**
- **½ teaspoon allspice dram liqueur**
- **2 oz. pineapple juice**
- **¾ oz. Coco López Cream of Coconut**
- **½ oz. orange juice**

1. Combine all of the ingredients in a cocktail shaker filled with ice and shake.
2. Strain the cocktail into a parfait glass, fill the glass with ice, and garnish with an orange slice and freshly grated nutmeg.

Banana-Infused Irish Whiskey: Chop 4 ripe bananas into 1-inch pieces and combine them with 1 (1 liter) bottle of Tullamore D.E.W. Allow the infusion to steep at room temperature for about 2 weeks. Strain several times and rebottle, making sure to not press spent bananas too much.

ROSÉ CHEEKS

THE JONES OYSTER CO.
22 EAST COURT STREET, GREENVILLE

The newest restaurant from the Table 301 team, The Jones Oyster Co. was popular from the moment it opened its doors, what with Greenville clamoring for plates of oysters and lobster rolls and lots of mineral-driven white wines to go along with them. However, the hits don't stop there; Jones has an excellent cocktail program designed to accompany all that shellfish too, including Spritzes like this one, created by Emma DeSollar and utilizing two of the South's favorites: rosé and Cathead Honeysuckle Vodka.

GLASSWARE: **Wineglass**

GARNISH: **Skewered orange peel and dried apricot**

- **1 oz. Cathead Honeysuckle Vodka**
- **½ oz. Rothman & Winter Orchard Apricot Liqueur**
- **1 oz. pink cranberry juice**
- **3 oz. brut rosé**

1. Fill a wineglass halfway with ice and add the vodka, liqueur, and juice.
2. Slowly stream in the rosé, then garnish with a skewered orange peel and dried apricot.

TRAPPE DOOR WHISKEY SOUR

TRAPPE DOOR
23 WEST WASHINGTON STREET, GREENVILLE

Trappe Door opened in 2011 and was an early catalyst for the downtown Greenville bar scene that was to come. Located in a basement space with an entrance on Washington Street, it's primarily known for Belgian food and a wide selection of craft beers, but through the years, a passionate group of bartenders has developed a strong craft cocktail game here too, including this peppery Whiskey Sour take from Mandy Covington that's easy to replicate and will open up a world of sour in your own cocktail game.

GLASSWARE: **Stemmed rocks glass**
GARNISH: **5 drops Vanilla Bourbon (see recipe)**

- **2 oz. Old Forester 86 Proof Bourbon**
- **¾ oz. Lemon-Pepper Syrup (see recipe)**
- **¾ oz. fresh lemon juice**
- **1 oz. egg white**

1. Combine all of the ingredients in a cocktail shaker and dry shake (without ice) for 10 to 20 seconds to create a froth.
2. Add ice and shake for another round to chill and dilute.
3. Double strain the cocktail into a stemmed rocks glass, then garnish with 5 drops Vanilla Bourbon.

Lemon-Pepper Syrup: In a saucepan over medium-high heat, combine 3 cups water, 3 cups sugar, 6 lemon peels, and 50 grams whole peppercorns, coarsely cracked, and bring the mixture to a boil. Lower the heat and simmer for about 30 minutes. Allow the syrup to cool, then strain it though a fine-mesh strainer and bottle.

Vanilla Bourbon: Combine 8 to 10 whole Madagascar vanilla beans and 1 (1 liter) bottle of bourbon in a large glass jar and allow the mixture to infuse for 1 month. Strain and rebottle.

OK

MEZCALUNA

BAR MARGARET
1269 PENDLETON STREET, GREENVILLE

Bar Margaret's cocktail program is one of the most progressive in Greenville, despite (or because of) the fact that they serve it alongside smashburgers and fries; have minimal garnishes, allowing the drinks to speak for themselves; and eschew any mention of the word "speakeasy." Instead, they have a come one, come all aesthetic with tables in the front of the restaurant, and a bar in the back where this cocktail has been a staple since it opened. It's a riff on the Bella Luna from *Death & Co: Modern Classic Cocktails*, but here, mezcal and crème de violette join in a smoky dance.

GLASSWARE: Nick & Nora glass

- **1½ oz. Pelotón de la Muerte**
- **¾ oz. St-Germain Elderflower Liqueur**
- **¼ oz. Rothman & Winter Crème de Violette**
- **½ oz. fresh lemon juice**

1. Chill a Nick & Nora glass. Combine all of the ingredients in a cocktail shaker filled with ice and shake well.
2. Double strain the cocktail into the chilled Nick & Nora.

THE TRAVELER

DRIFTWOOD
12 LOIS AVENUE, GREENVILLE

Driftwood, primarily a wine bar in West Greenville, has a serious cocktail program, and when the weather is fine, they lift the garage doors for a lovely open-air feel. The first night this happens is a quiet cause for celebration, and this cocktail is the perfect way to toast to warmer days ahead. The elements of the Negroni are all here, but the absinthe muddles the Italian accent, in much the same way a traveler can start to sound after too long away from his home of origin.

GLASSWARE: **Martini glass**

GARNISH: **Orange peel**

- **Absinthe, to rinse**
- **2 oz. Lustau Vermut Rojo**
- **½ oz. Citadelle Original Gin**
- **½ oz. Campari**
- **4 dashes Peychaud's bitters**

1. Rinse a martini glass with absinthe.
2. Combine the remaining ingredients in a cocktail shaker filled with ice and shake.
3. Strain the cocktail into the rinsed glass and garnish with an orange peel.

THE LADY DIANA

SOBY'S
207 SOUTH MAIN STREET, GREENVILLE

Soby's is, now close to thirty years in, a Greenville institution, and in many ways the catalyst for what this Upstate city's hospitality scene has now become. It's a place to celebrate, for sure, but for many locals, the bar was and is an extended front porch of sorts. This cocktail, created in honor of a beloved guest named Diana DeCastro, illustrates this. She and Brandon Urrego, Soby's bartender, built a great kinship through the years, and after her death, he wanted to honor her. Therefore, he created this floral, fruity cocktail in her favorite color—yellow—and added it to the menu. Now Diana is remembered every time the cocktail is ordered.

GLASSWARE: **Coupe glass**
GARNISH: **Edible flower**

- **1 oz. Tito's Handmade Vodka**
- **1 oz. fresh lime juice**
- **½ oz. mango puree**
- **½ oz. water**
- **⅓ oz. St-Germain Elderflower Liqueur**
- **⅓ oz. Giffard Banane du Brésil**
- **⅓ oz. Giffard Abricot du Roussillon**

1. Combine all of the ingredients in a cocktail shaker with ice and shake.
2. Double strain the cocktail into a coupe and garnish with an edible flower.

SUMMER LOVIN

THE 07
1010 LAURENS ROAD, GREENVILLE

Jeni Blyth is a well-known figure in Greenville cocktail culture, from competitions to Saturday nights working the service bar. She recently joined the team at The 07, a neighborhood restaurant by the team of Geno Iozzino and Anmar Natheer, who also own The 05 on Augusta Street, and she brings a forward-thinking sensibility to the neighborhood cocktail spot. Here, she keeps it light and breezy.

GLASSWARE: Nick & Nora glass
GARNISH: Lime-peel bird

- **1½ oz. Conniption Kinship Gin**
- **¾ oz. Italicus Rosolio di Bergamotto**
- **¾ oz. Lime Cordial (see recipe)**
- **3 drops rose water**

1. Combine all of the ingredients in a cocktail shaker filled with ice and shake.
2. Double strain the cocktail into a Nick & Nora and garnish with a decorative lime-peel bird.

LIME CORDIAL: Zest and juice 2 limes, then combine the zest and juice with 1 cup sugar, 1 cup hot water, and 25 grams citric acid in a blender and blend on medium for 30 seconds. Fine strain, bottle, and store the cordial in the refrigerator.

Lemon Foam: Dissolve 1½ sheets gelatin in 5 oz. warm water. Add 3 oz. egg whites; 2¼ oz. Simple Syrup (see recipe on page 20), steeped with lemon peels; and 2¼ oz. fresh lemon juice. Pour the mixture into an iSi canister, charge twice, and shake vigorously.

SIR PERCY

SCOUNDREL
18 NORTH MAIN STREET, GREENVILLE

Scoundrel is a French-inspired eatery on Main Street where Francophilia often extends to the bar program. Named after the protagonist from the 1905 novel The Scarlet Pimpernel—whom Joe Cash of Scoundrel refers to as the "James Bond of the French Revolution"—this fluffy-frocked White Negroni looks like it's hiding a dark secret under frilly sleeve cuffs; it's meant to be enjoyed before the drink warms and the foam flattens. Percy would certainly approve.

GLASSWARE: Coupe glass
GARNISH: Lemon peel

- **1 oz. Conniption Navy Strength Gin**
- **½ oz. Dolin Dry Vermouth**
- **½ oz. Dolin Blanc Vermouth**
- **½ oz. Cocchi Americano**
- **½ oz. Italicus Rosolio di Bergamotto**
- **Lemon Foam (see recipe), to top**

1. Combine all of the ingredients, except for the foam, in a mixing glass filled with ice and stir.
2. Strain the cocktail into a coupe, top with Lemon Foam, and garnish with a lemon peel.

DEW BEGINNING

CAMP
2 EAST BROAD STREET, GREENVILLE

Scotch is actually versatile but often gets pigeonholed into the woolen-socks part of winter. Here, CAMP showcases it in between summer and fall, offering refreshment but with some heft for cool nights when it's still comfortable enough to sit at the restaurant's popular outdoor bar. This cocktail has a robust, round base from the scotch, with hints of bitter herbaceousness and a citrus kick, and as a bonus, it's a great way to bring Aperol beyond Spritz season.

GLASSWARE: **Rocks glass**
GARNISH: **Dehydrated orange slice**

- **1½ oz. Dewar's White Label Blended Scotch Whisky**
- **½ oz. Aperol**
- **½ oz. fresh lemon juice**
- **¼ oz. Licor 43**
- **¼ oz. Fig and Cardamom Syrup (see recipe)**
- **3 dashes orange bitters**

1. Combine all of the ingredients in a cocktail shaker filled with ice and shake.
2. Strain the cocktail into a rocks glass over a large ice cube and garnish with a dehydrated orange slice.

Fig and Cardamom Syrup: In a pot over medium heat, combine ¼ cup sugar and ¼ cup water to make a simple syrup. Pour the syrup over ¼ cup fig jam and ¼ cup cardamom pods and stir to combine. Steep for 4 to 6 hours. Strain and store the syrup in an airtight container in the refrigerator for up to 1 month.

THE GOLDEN HOUR

MR. CRISP
1501 EAST NORTH STREET, SUITE 102, GREENVILLE

Mr. Crisp, located in the Overbrook neighborhood, is the more casual sister restaurant to The Anchorage. Bar manager Andy Rhine is well-known for highly crafted cocktails, including The Golden Hour, a milk-clarified bourbon cocktail that must be made in a large batch. What makes this style of cocktail so attractive for modern bartenders is the crystal clear results and creamy texture that remains after straining. The lactose proteins curdle with the lime acid in a delicious science experiment that results in a party-size portion. This batch serves eight; just make sure that each glass is garnished with a turmeric rim.

GLASSWARE: **Nick & Nora glasses**

- **Turmeric, for the rim**
- **16 oz. Four Roses Bourbon**
- **4 oz. St. Elizabeth Allspice Dram**
- **6 oz. fresh lime juice**
- **⅓ cup Cinnamon Cordial**
- **½ oz. Angostura bitters**
- **½ oz. saline**
- **¼ total volume of ingredients above of whole milk**

1. Combine all of the ingredients, except for the tumeric, in a large container with a lid and allow the mixture to sit overnight in the refrigerator.
2. Wet the rim of a Nick & Nora glass, then dip the glass in turmeric to give it a rim.
3. Using a fine-mesh strainer with a coffee filter in it, strain off the milk solids and pour each serving into a rimmed glass.

CINNAMON CORDIAL: In a pot over medium heat, combine 1 pint water, 1 pint turbinado sugar, and 8 cinnamon sticks and simmer for 30 minutes. Remove the syrup from heat and allow it to cool. Remove the cinnamon sticks, add 2 drops vanilla extract, and stir. Store the cordial in an airtight container for up to 1 month.

POOR LITTLE RICH GIRL

SWORDFISH COCKTAIL CLUB
220 EAST COFFEE STREET, GREENVILLE

Swordfish Cocktail Club is just the sort of place where not only would they have heard of the classic cocktail Mary Pickford, but they would also know it well enough to give it a fresh take when a customer requests it. For this cocktail, Evan Leihy substituted orange and lime juice for fresh pineapple juice—a key ingredient in the original—and included pineapple rum, which enhanced the drink's top notes. The guest was thrilled, stating that it surpassed the original, and Swordfish put it on the menu soon after, naming it after a film in which the actress starred: *The Poor Little Rich Girl.*

GLASSWARE: Coupe glass

GARNISH: Lime peel, expressed; skewered Luxardo cherry

- **2 oz. Planteray Stiggins' Fancy Pineapple Rum**
- **1 oz. orange juice**
- **½ oz. fresh lime juice**
- **½ oz. grenadine**
- **¼ oz. Luxardo Maraschino Originale**

1. Chill a coupe glass. Combine all of the ingredients in a cocktail shaker filled with ice and shake.
2. Double strain the cocktail into the chilled coupe.
3. Express a lime peel over the glass and add it and a skewered Luxardo cherry as garnishes.

AUDREY II

THE CAZBAH
16 WEST MCBEE AVENUE, GREENVILLE

Sunday night at The Cazbah is unofficially food and beverage night. Hospitality workers from all over the Greenville area come to the West McBee spot for camaraderie, fried wonton lobster cigars, and stellar cocktails such as this one, which is a reviver of sorts, based on a popular Mexican juice blend. Audrey II is a double entendre, both referencing *The Little Shop of Horrors* and the owner's name, and although it was originally created during the Halloween season, it offers refreshment year-round.

GLASSWARE: **Rocks glass**
GARNISH: **Flower, sprinkle of Tajín**

- **1¼ oz. Tequila Ocho Plata**
- **1¼ oz. Veriditas Juice (see recipe)**
- **½ oz. Pierre Ferrand Dry Curaçao**
- **¼ oz. Habanero-Infused Agave Syrup (see recipe)**

1. Combine all of the ingredients in a cocktail shaker filled with ice and shake.
2. Strain the cocktail into a rocks glass with a big ice cube and garnish with a flower and a sprinkle of Tajín on the ice.

Veriditas Juice: In a blender, combine 1 (46 oz.) can of pineapple juice, 1 bunch of cilantro, ½ bunch of mint, and 3 jalapeños, then store the juice in an airtight container in the refrigerator for up to 1 week.

Habanero-Infused Agave Syrup: Combine 16 oz. agave nectar; 3 habanero peppers, chopped; and ½ oz. mezcal in a container, stir to incorporate, and then allow the infusion to sit and macerate for 4 to 6 hours. Strain and rebottle.

BLUEBERRY LIMONCELLO MARTINI

THE CAPTAIN AT HOTEL HARTNESS
120 HALSTON AVENUE, GREENVILLE

Although Josh Hamlin, director of banquets for Hotel Hartness, originally created the cocktail to pay homage to the Tuscan countryside, it's more fitting that this boutique hotel bar is set in the suburbs of Greenville, because blueberries are a well-known Upstate crop. Purchase blueberry puree anytime from a company such as Monin, or in season, pick and puree your own.

GLASSWARE: Martini glass
GARNISH: Lemon peel

- **2 oz. Grey Goose Vodka**
- **1 oz. Pallini Limoncello**
- **1 oz. blueberry puree**

1. Chill a martini glass. Combine all of the ingredients in a cocktail shaker filled with ice and shake.
2. Strain the cocktail into the chilled martini glass and garnish with a lemon peel.

RHUBARBRA

TOPSOIL
13 SOUTH MAIN STREET, TRAVELERS REST

When Kristin Binns's wife returned from France recalling a light rhubarb-based cocktail that included baie de timut pepper, the bar manager knew she wanted to re-create it. "Working at a place as farm connected as Topsoil, we often get access to ingredients your average restaurant wouldn't choose to or simply couldn't, such as rhubarb," she says. While she wasn't able to source the fragrant ingredient—the pepper grows wild in Nepal and is now used in much of Asia—pink peppercorn was a worthy substitute. What results is a cocktail that looks dainty yet packs a wonderful punch.

GLASSWARE: Coupe glass

GARNISH: Pinch pink peppercorns

- **1½ oz. Ketel One Vodka**
- **1½ oz. Rhubarb Liqueur (see recipe)**
- **½ oz. Pink Peppercorn Syrup (see recipe)**
- **½ oz. fresh lemon juice**
- **1 egg white**

1. Combine all of the ingredients, except for the egg white, with ice and shake.
2. Strain the cocktail into the smaller shaker tin.
3. Add the egg white, combine the shakers again, and shake for at least 30 seconds, until you no longer hear ice chips and can feel some pressure.
4. Strain the cocktail into a coupe and garnish with a pinch of pink peppercorns.

RHUBARB LIQUEUR: Combine 2 pounds washed, chopped rhubarb stems and 1½ cups sugar in a large, sealable jar and shake. Cover the rhubarb completely with 1 (750 ml) bottle of vodka and allow the infusion to sit somewhere dark and cool, but not refrigerated, for 4 to 6 weeks, shaking the jar occasionally, until the color is leached from the stalks. Strain and rebottle.

PINK PEPPERCORN SYRUP: In a saucepan over medium heat, toast whole peppercorns, as needed, for 1 to 2 minutes, until fragrant but not burning. Add 1 cup water and bring it to a boil. Add 1 cup sugar, stir, and return to a boil. Remove the syrup from heat, let it cool, and then strain.

BAJA BLAST

NU-WAY LOUNGE & RESTAURANT
373 EAST KENNEDY STREET, SPARTANBURG

There are vintage Budweiser chandeliers, no windows, and a really good cheeseburger, so it's unimaginable to skip Nu-Way on a tour of Spartanburg cocktail culture, especially since they've been serving up the suds and sips for the Spartanburg community since 1938. This cocktail is currently one of their most popular, and it illustrates that they do, in fact, change with the times. It's a nod to a Taco Bell beverage of the same name, but in reality, it's a kissing cousin to a Long Island Iced Tea (in a pretty blue jacket), so sip accordingly.

GLASSWARE: **Pint glass**
GARNISH: **Orange slice**

- **¾ oz. Lunazul Tequila Blanco**
- **¾ oz. Smirnoff Raspberry**
- **¾ oz. Malibu Original rum**
- **¾ oz. peach schnapps**
- **¾ oz. sour mix**
- **¾ oz. pineapple juice**
- **¼ oz. Rose's Sweetened Lime Juice**
- **¼ oz. blue curaçao**
- **Sprite, to top**

1. Fill a pint glass with ice and add all of the ingredients in the order listed.
2. Garnish with an orange slice.

THE TIRAMISU COCKTAIL

RICK ERWIN'S LEVEL 10
AC HOTEL SPARTANBURG, 225 WEST MAIN STREET, UNIT 100, SPARTANBURG

More dessert than drink, this cocktail is one of the most popular offerings at Rick Erwin's Level 10, a rooftop steak house in the AC Hotel. There's a dress code, a seafood tower, and a béarnaise sauce add-on option for your filet, so decadence is the name of the game. This creamy cocktail includes RumChata (a liqueur popular in South Carolina bottle shops that is a mix of cream, rum, and spices) and is, of course, modeled after the popular Italian dessert. It's a fitting stand-in for one.

GLASSWARE: Coupe glass
GARNISH: Cocoa powder

- **1½ oz. Mozart Chocolate Cream Liqueur**
- **1½ oz. Kahlúa**
- **1½ oz. RumChata**

1. Combine all of the ingredients in a cocktail tin filled with ice and shake vigorously.
2. Strain and pour the cocktail into a coupe, and garnish with cocoa powder.

Blackberry Shrub: In a container, muddle together 1 cup blackberries and 1 cup sugar, then stir in 1 cup apple cider vinegar or white wine vinegar. Cover and store the shrub in the refrigerator for 3 to 5 days. Fine strain and rebottle the shrub, and keep it in the refrigerator until ready to use.

EL CHUPACABRA

ISLA'S ON THE SQUARE
113 NORTH CHURCH STREET, SPARTANBURG

Mezcal gin or agave gin is a frontier spirits category at the moment, with a few producers using agave to create something that has the herbaceous and floral notes of gin with a hint of smoke. The brands available are small batch (read pricey) but sincerely unique, and in this cocktail created by co–bar manager Matthew Albertson, the spirit's revolutionary ways help bring together elements that seem disparate on paper. The result is a deeply fruity and floral standout in the Spartanburg cocktail landscape.

GLASSWARE: Tiki mug
GARNISH: Mint sprig

- **1½ oz. Mezcal Gin**
- **½ oz. Chinola Passion Fruit Liqueur**
- **¼ oz. fresh lime juice**
- **1 oz. Blackberry Shrub (see recipe)**
- **1 oz. dry red wine, to top**

1. Combine all of the ingredients, except for the red wine, in a cocktail shaker filled with ice and shake.
2. Strain the mixture over fresh ice into a tiki mug.
3. Float the red wine on top for a vibrant finish, and garnish with a mint sprig.

Photo Credits

Pages 16, 113 Basic Projects; page 27 Alison Rourk; pages 29, 100 Peter Frank Edwards; page 33 Ashley Hay Mitchell; pages 35, 36 Stephen Blackmon; pages 45, 46, 52, 60, 103, 224 Andrew Cebulka; pages 49, 262 Leigh-Ann Beverley; page 51 Jai Jones; page 64 Nadya Hutson; page 67 Aleece Sophia; page 71 Lizzy Rollins; page 77 Timmy Nguyen; page 79 Squire Fox; page 85 Alexander Duffy; page 99 Megan Madaris; page 104 Kate Kirby; page 106 Kiawah Island Golf Resort; page 109 Zach Thompson; page 110 Jonathan Boncek; page 115 Jessica Backus; page 118 Maddy Goyal; page 123 Eastwoods Media; page 137 Eva Moore; pages 140, 147, 159 Forrest Clonts; page 143 Heather Hill; pages 144, 152 City Social; pages 148, 160 Lynn Luc; page 164 Blake Pope; page 167 Kounter; page 170 Daly Pardue; page 179 True Light Photography; pages 181, 220 Indigo Road Hospitality; page 185 TJ Brister; page 186 Natasha Sprinkle; page 190 Tracy A. Smith; page 193 Jacob Vasquez; pages 202–203 Jonathan Cooper; page 209 Kevin Sanfilippo; pages 213, 214 Parkkonen Photography; page 216 Adam Kirwan; page 219 Ridge Media; page 227 Michael Grissinger; pages 228, 236, 242 Table 301 Restaurant Group; page 240 Savannah Bockus, Max DiNatale Digital Marketing; page 246 Hanah Molina; page 253 Katie Chaney; page 257 Caitie Wade; page 258 Morgan Square Hospitality Group.

Pages 30, 55, 56, 59, 75, 80, 83, 86, 89, 90, 93, 94, 97, 131, 139, 155, 156, 163, 189, 194, 199, 200, 210, 223, 231, 232, 239, 245, 250, 254 by Stephanie Burt.

Pages 1, 3, 4–5, 6, 22–23, 56–57, 132–133, 172–173, 177, 204–205 used under official license from Shutterstock.com.

Pages 7, 8, 10, courtesy of the Library of Congress.

All other images courtesy of the respective bars, restaurants, and interviewees.

Acknowledgments

Thank you to Ann Marshall and Scott Blackwell for their years of education and introductions in the American craft beverage space, and to Matt and Ted Lee, Jai Jones, Richard Reutter, Debi Schadel, Moonbaby of Nu-Way, Zach Fox, Ivie Parker, Taryn Scher, Ariel Blanchard, John Ondo, Cat Taylor, Vonda Freeman, the team at Sprouthouse, Eric Gordon, Megan Deschaine, Janette Wesley, Charlie Clark, and each and every one of the beverage professionals and photographers featured here. Finally, a special thanks to family and friends who cheered me on and were willing to endure me waxing on about writing this book. I owe you all a drink.

About the Author

Stephanie Burt is a writer, multimedia producer, and sometimes cook based in Charleston, South Carolina. Her work has appeared in numerous publications, including *Saveur*, *The Washington Post*, CNN's *Anthony Bourdain: Parts Unknown*, *Condé Nast Traveler*, and *The Bitter Southerner*, and she was the host and executive producer of the *Southern Fork* podcast for nine seasons.

MEASUREMENT CONVERSIONS

	1 dash		0.625 ml
	4 dashes		2.5 ml
	1 teaspoon		5 ml
¼ oz.			7.5 ml
⅓ oz.	2 teaspoons		10 ml
½ oz.	3 teaspoons	1 tablespoon	15 ml
⅔ oz.	4 teaspoons		20 ml
¾ oz.			22.5 ml
17/20 oz.			25 ml
1 oz.		2 tablespoons	30 ml
1½ oz.		3 tablespoons	45 ml
1¾ oz.			52.5 ml
2 oz.	4 tablespoons	¼ cup	60 ml
8 oz.		1 cup	250 ml
16 oz.	1 pint	2 cups	500 ml
24 oz.		3 cups	750 ml
32 oz.	1 quart	4 cups	1 liter (1,000 ml)

Index

–About Cider Mill Press Book Publishers–

Cider Mill Press publishes exceptional books that combine creativity and craftsmanship. As an imprint of HarperCollins Focus, we specialize in premium cookbooks, cocktail and spirits guides, and illustrated gift books, all distinguished by compelling content, striking design, and a commitment to quality in every detail. Cider Mill Press sets the standard for books that inform, inspire, and elevate everyday moments. Learn more at cidermillpress.com.

"Where Good Books Are Ready for Press"

501 Nelson Place
Nashville, Tennessee 37214

GREENWOOD
SALUDA
MC CORMICK
LEXINGTON
RICHLAN
EDGEFIELD
AIKEN
CALHO
ORANGEB
BARNWELL
BAMBERG
ALLENDALE
HAMPTON
COL
JASPER
BEA
G
I
A
CLARK HILL RESERVOIR
LAKE MURRAY
Par Pond
SAVANNAH RIVER
Greenwood
Abbeville
Columbia
West Columbia
Cayce
Lexington
Batesburg
Leesville
Saluda
Edgefield
Johnston
Trenton
McCormick
Aiken
North Augusta
Graniteville
Williston
Blackville
Denmark
Bamberg
Barnwell
Allendale
Hampton
Orangeburg
Ridgeland
Hardeeville
Jasper
Hilton Head Island
UNITED STATES
ENT OF THE INTERIOR
LOGICAL SURVEY
OUTH CAROLINA
Scale 1:500,000
um is mean sea level
SOURCE DATA
POPULATION KEY
COLUMBIA .... more than 50,000
ROCK HILL .... 25,000 to 50,000
Greenwood .... 10,000 to 25,000
Camden .... 2,500 to 10,000
Landrum .... less than 2,500
Population indicated by size of letters
BASE MAP
OGICAL SURVEY, WASHINGTON, D. C. 20242
COMPILED IN 1970
EDITION OF 1970

GREENWOOD
SALUDA
McCORMICK
LEXINGTON
COLUMBIA
RICHLAND
EDGEFIELD
CLARK HILL RESERVOIR
CALHOUN
AIKEN
North Augusta
Aiken
Orangeburg
ORANGEBURG
BARNWELL
Par Pond
BAMBERG
ALLENDALE
HAMPTON
JASPER
SAVANNAH RIVER
UNITED STATES
DEPARTMENT OF THE INTERIOR
GEOLOGICAL SURVEY
SOUTH CAROLINA
Scale 1:500,000
1 inch equals approximately 8 miles
Datum is mean sea level
POPULATION KEY
COLUMBIA .... more than 50,000
ROCK HILL .... 25,000 to 50,000
Greenwood .... 10,000 to 25,000
Camden .... 2,500 to 10,000
Landrum .... less than 2,500
SOURCE DATA
BASE MAP
GEOLOGICAL SURVEY, WASHINGTON, D. C. 20242
COMPILED IN 1970
EDITION OF 1970